Old Alyth
John Alexander

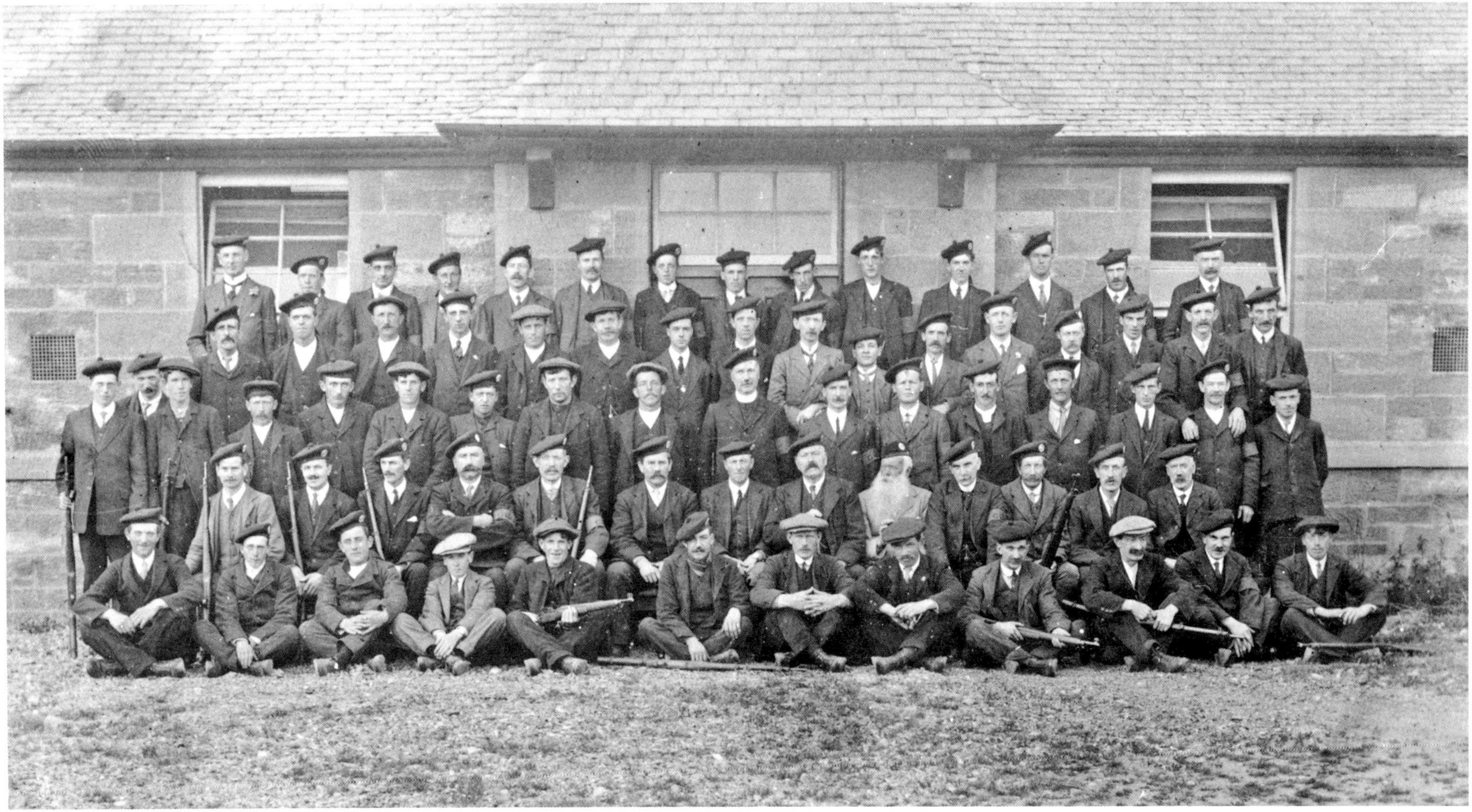

Most of these men are wearing bonnets, none are in uniform and only a few have weapons, but a hand-written note on the back of this picture describes them as the Alyth Volunteers during the Great War 1914-1918.

© John Alexander, 2022
First published in the United Kingdom, 2022,
by Stenlake Publishing Ltd.
www.stenlake.co.uk
ISBN 978-1-84033-949-9

The publishers regret that they cannot supply copies of any pictures featured in this book.

Printed by
Claro Print, Office 26, 27, 1 Spiersbridge Way,
Thornliebank, Glasgow G46 8NG

Acknowledgements

Having compiled a little book about Glenisla, Lintrathen and Airlie in 2020, during the Covid 19 pandemic, it seemed like a good idea to follow that up with a similar volume for Alyth. As ever life is never that simple and because these have been difficult years it has taken a while to put the plan into action, but happily it has now come to fruition. As with Glenisla, it has been a delight to delve into the stories that have gone into making up these pages, not a definitive or comprehensive history, but hopefully an enjoyable trip into aspects of Alyth's past.

Further Reading

The following were the principal books used by the author during his research.

Alyth Town Council: Alyth Official Guide, undated *c.*1950s.
Haynes, Nick, Perth & Kinross, an illustrated architectural guide, 2000.
Hutchinson, Dave, A Braw Toon for Messages, 2007.
Norrie, James Ltd., Official Guide To Alyth, 1961.
Thomas, John and Turnock, David, A Regional History of the Railways of Great Britain, Vol. 15 North of Scotland, 1989.

Websites

As well as consulting subject-specific sites, valuable information also came through more general ones, namely:

British Newspaper Archive.
Cateran Ecomuseum.
Historic Environment Scotland: Scotland's Places, and Canmore.
Dictionary of Scottish Architects.
National Library of Scotland: NLS Maps.
Scottish Church Heritage Research: Places of Worship in Scotland.

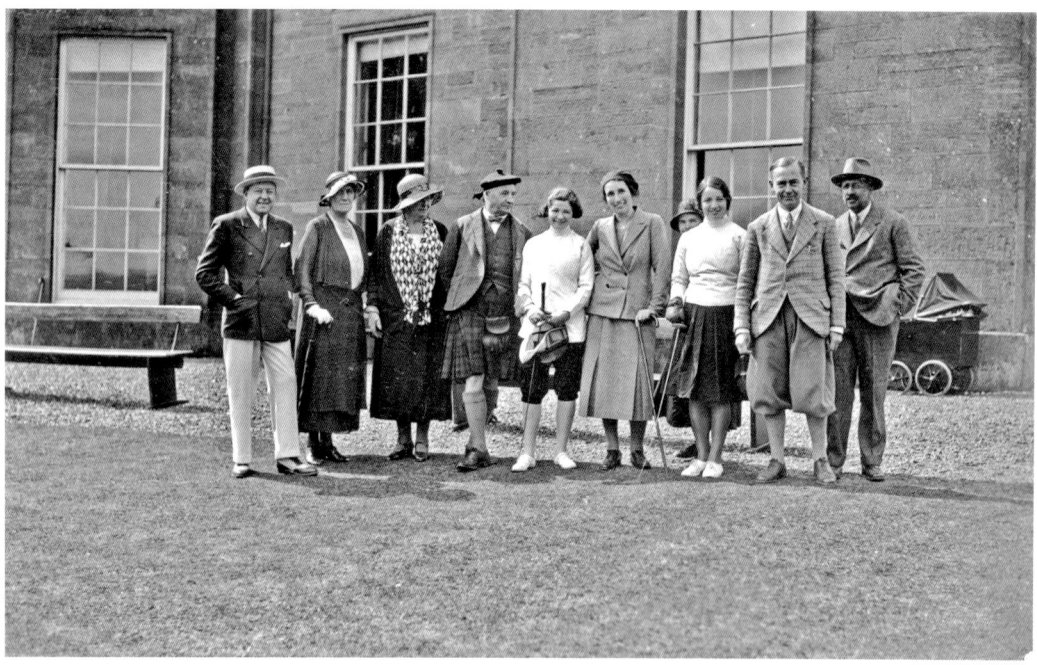

Included in this group photographed outside Balhary House at the summer solstice in 1933 are two young women apparently equipped for the sport of fencing.

Introduction

Alyth is a small market town set amongst grand scenery. To the south is Strathmore, the big valley, and to the north the majestic Grampian Mountains. Burns running off the slopes pour down many small glens and combine to form the splendid River Isla, which flows then roars down its own larger glen. Between Glen Isla and Glen Shee, to the west, is the extensive Forest of Alyth, once a favoured Royal hunting ground. Commanding the foot of Glen Isla, Airlie Castle, 'The Bonnie Hoose o' Airlie', stood tall until the Earl of Argyll destroyed it in 1640, but the Ogilvy family, the Earls of Airlie, retained it and extensive lands in the surrounding area. Lying to the south and west of the castle, Alyth is like an anchor for the glen, providing a market for its produce and in later years acting as its post town.

The old town with its church and market place was situated on high ground to the north. There, well above the flood-prone burn, the ground was dry, but as the town began to move south, the water was tamed between stone banks and the old town declined. New streets were laid out alongside the burn and on the west bank what amounted to a new town was built with Airlie Street as its spine.

The burn was at the heart of changing times as weirs were built to divert its flow to drive mills. There was a corn mill, but textiles were the main industry, prompted by state initiatives to encourage development of the linen trade, though jute and wool also featured. Despite its good power source, Alyth was at a disadvantage in the developing world of nineteenth century industry. It was close to the big textile centre of Dundee, but roads were poor and transport was difficult until railways pushed north initially to Newtyle and then, after a thirty year wait, into Alyth. The town's fortunes were transformed and it changed physically too, continuing its shift south in the direction of the new station.

The railway also inspired a new industry as travel operators and hoteliers sought to exploit Alyth's potential for tourism, extolling the area's scenic delights and bracing country air. The textile mills eventually closed, but the one industry that never faltered was agriculture with farms large and small jostling with country houses and their policies for space in the landscape. Some of those big houses have also gone, while the bucolic image of a timeless countryside is disappearing in the face of farm mechanisation.

In common with market towns across the country that no longer hold markets, Alyth has adapted to a changing world in which its position at the centre of scenic splendour also puts it at the heart of a landscape creatively packaged for visitors keen to explore a range of historic and environmental experiences. The nature of tourism may have changed, but Alyth's attractions are timeless.

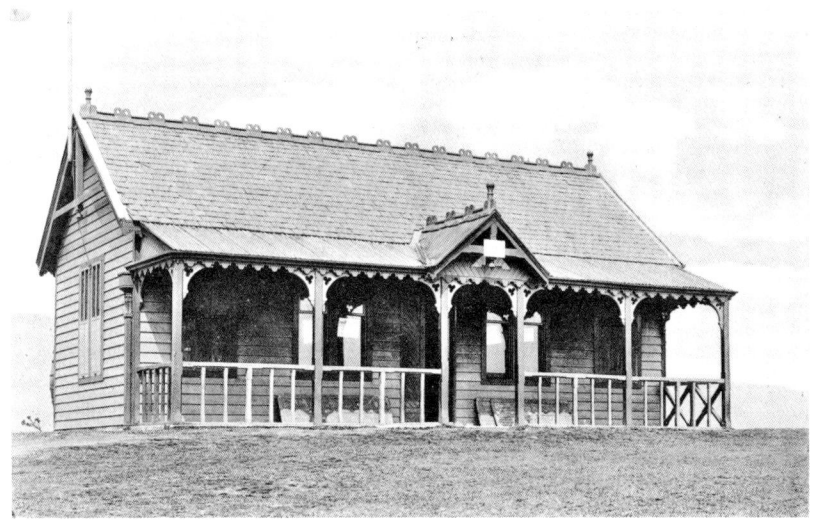

The golf clubhouse has been significantly upgraded since this early model graced the course at Pitcrocknie.

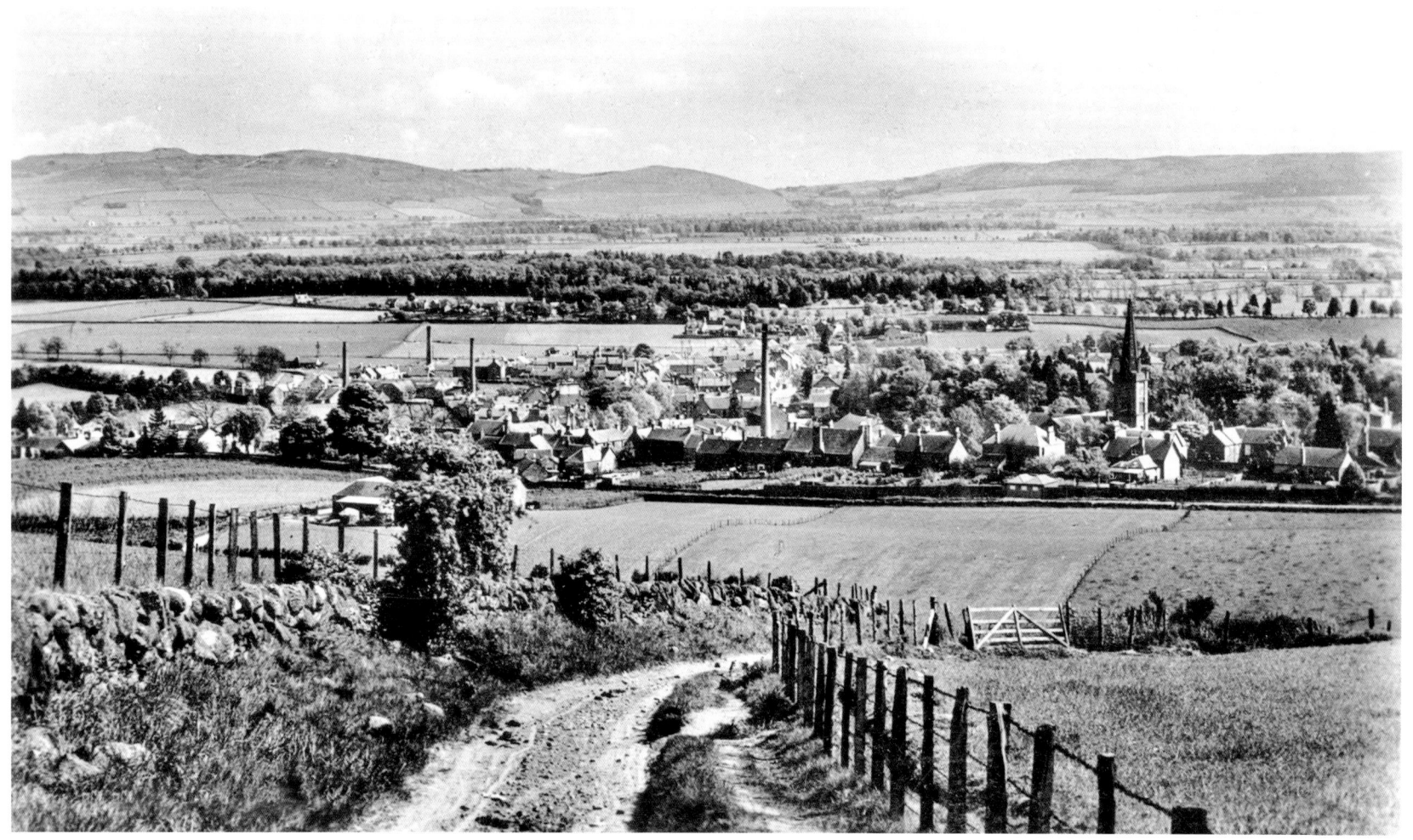

With Strathmore and the Sidlaw Hills in the distance, Alyth is seen here in 1930 looking south from the Hill of Alyth, one of three heights that lie to the north of the town. To its east is the Hill of Loyal and further east Barry Hill, the site of a large ancient fort. It is made up of many ramparts and, although now overgrown, there is evidence that some of the stones have been fused together by heat. Early antiquarians used to describe such structures as vitrified forts believing that the fusing was a deliberate construction technique, but the more modern interpretation is that the fort walls were made with rubble stones held in place by timber lacing and the fusing came about when the forts were attacked and burned. A structure on this scale is a clear indication that this corner of Perthshire has been inhabited for a very long time.

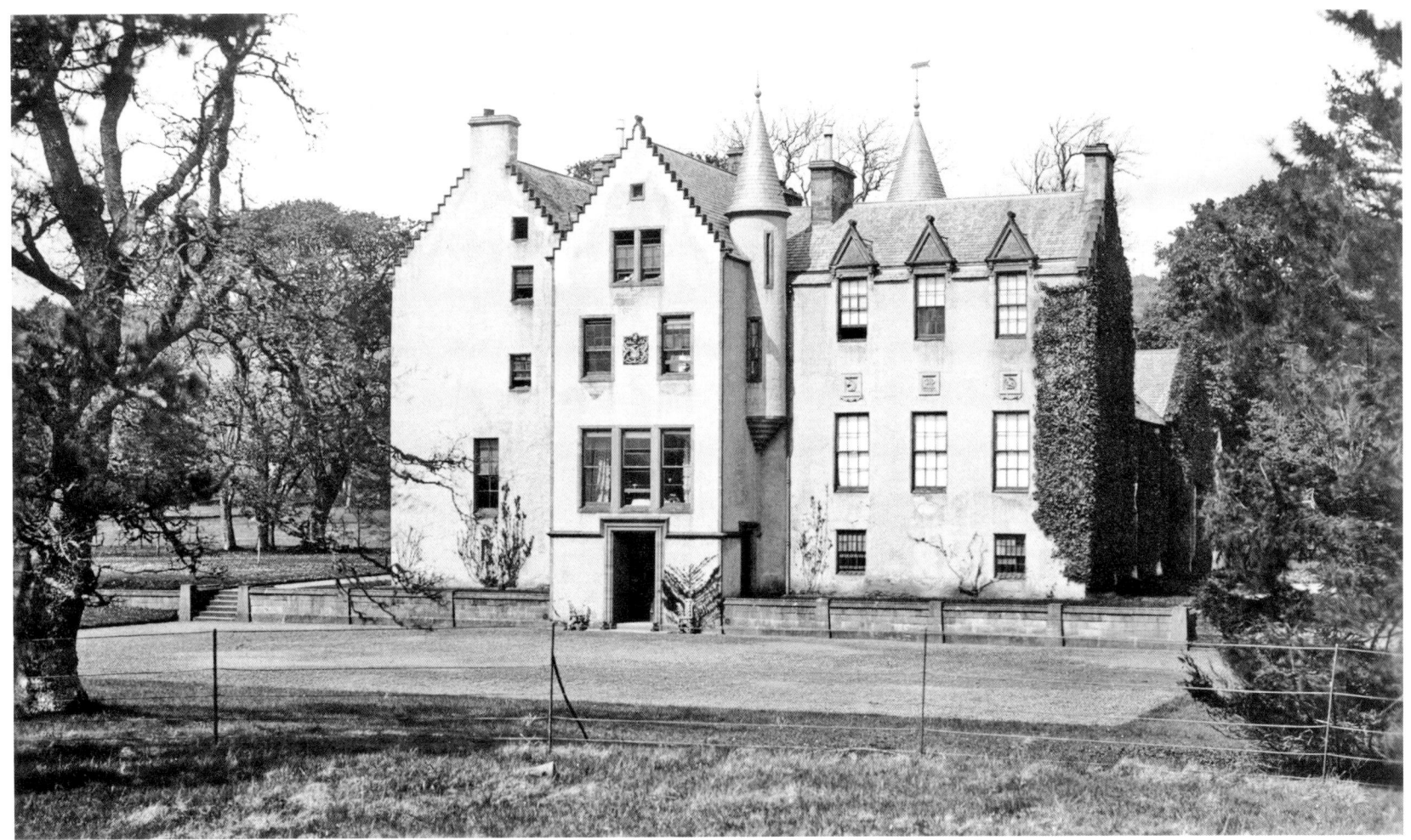

Tucked in behind the Hill of Alyth is another old structure, although not as ancient as the Barry Hill fort. Bamff House has been in existence in one form or another since the lands were granted to the physician, Neis, progenitor of the Ramsay family by King Alexander II in 1232. Situated on a rocky base surrounded by boggy ground, the later tower house was erected in *c.*1580-1595, probably building on the foundations of the earlier structure and incorporating parts of it. It was subsequently altered and extended in the 18th and 19th centuries. During the Second World War the house proved to be an ideal location for the branch of the women's land army engaged in forestry work known as 'lumberjills'. More recently, a population of beavers have been using a different method to fell trees.

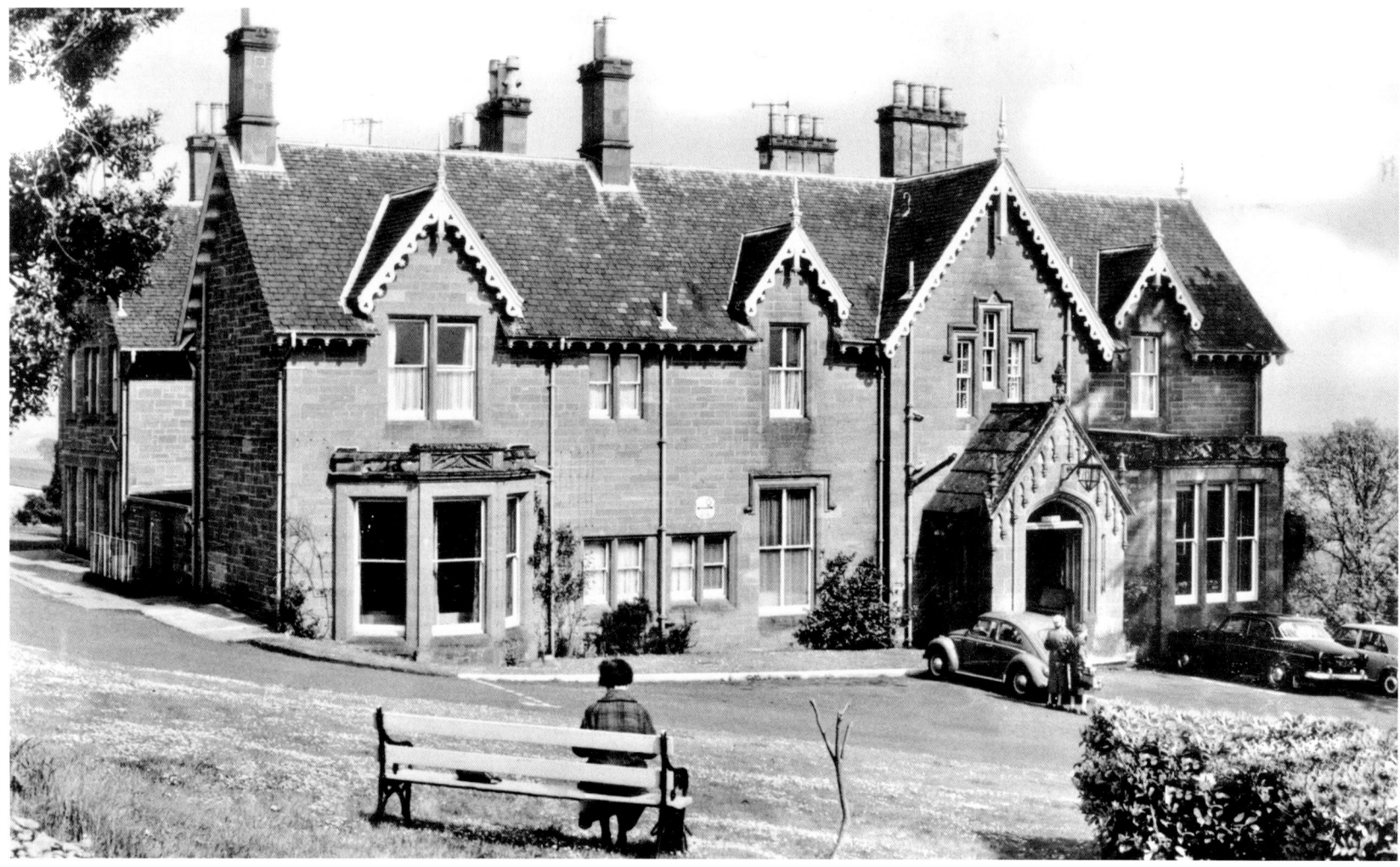

Nestling at the base of the Hill of Loyal, Loyal House was built in 1850 for the Hon. Captain William Ogilvy, brother of the 8th Earl of Airlie by Perth-based architect Andrew Heiton. It was enlarged in the late 1870s for a new owner but by 1945 it had ceased to be a private dwelling and became the Lands of Loyal Hotel set in its own private grounds. Seen here in the early 1960s, it initially had twenty bedrooms, all with hot and cold water, but not en-suite – the seven bathrooms were separate. There was central heating, garage accommodation, a small open-air swimming pool, tennis courts and a games room. Since those early days, when electricity was regarded as a unique selling point, the hotel has been significantly upgraded.

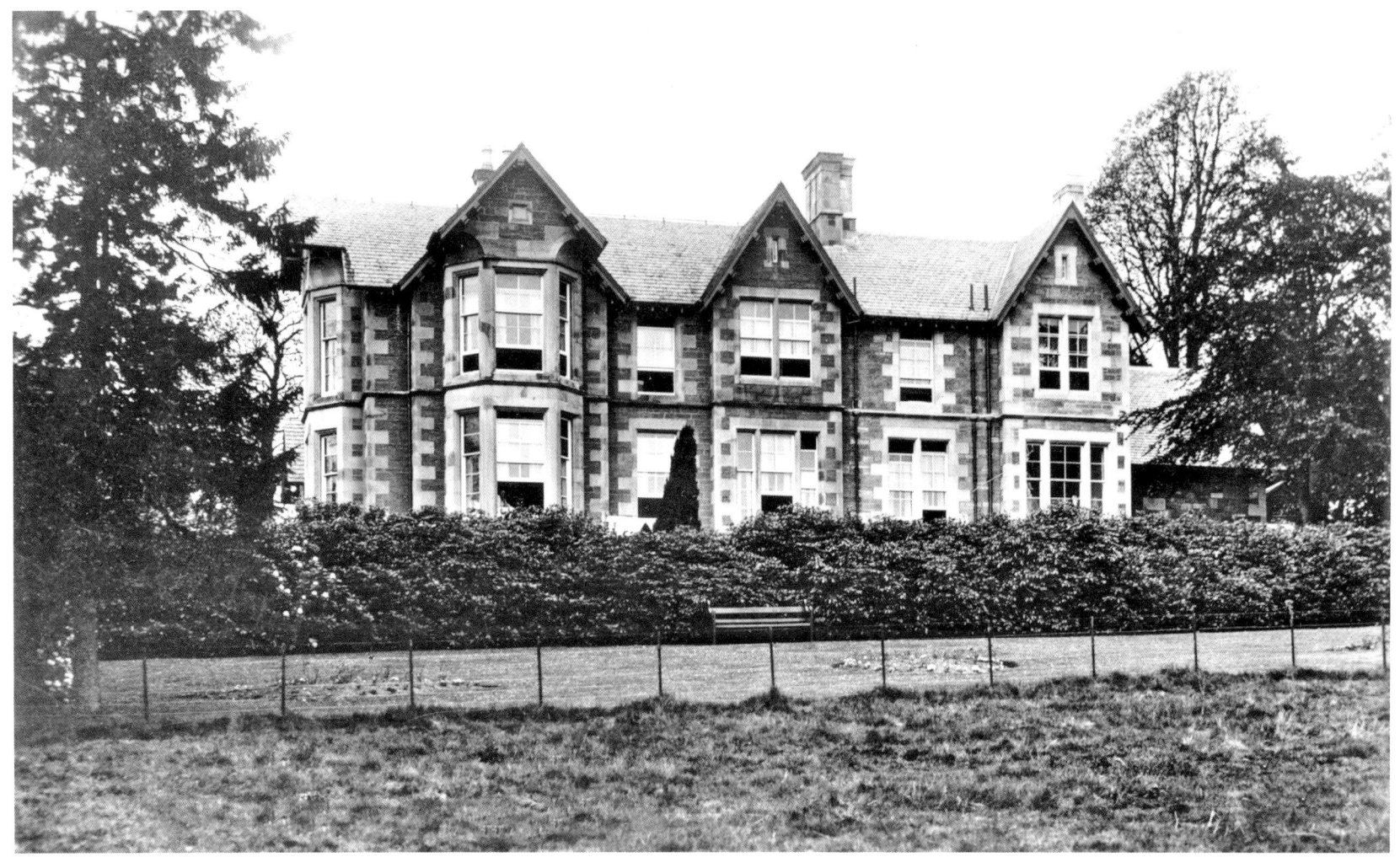

Just down the hill from Loyal House was Viewfield Villa, a large Victorian house that was purchased in 1921 by Andrew Cochrane of Craigisla and James H. Fyfe Jamieson of Ruthven. They gifted the building to Alyth, Meigle and District Nursing Association for use as a nursing home, maternity hospital and home for disabled children. The Dowager Countess of Airlie opened it in October 1922 as View Park Nursing Home. It ceased to operate as a maternity home in 1964 when a new facility was opened in Blairgowrie, but remained in use as a short-term health care facility. That function had ceased when it was converted back into domestic accommodation in 2014.

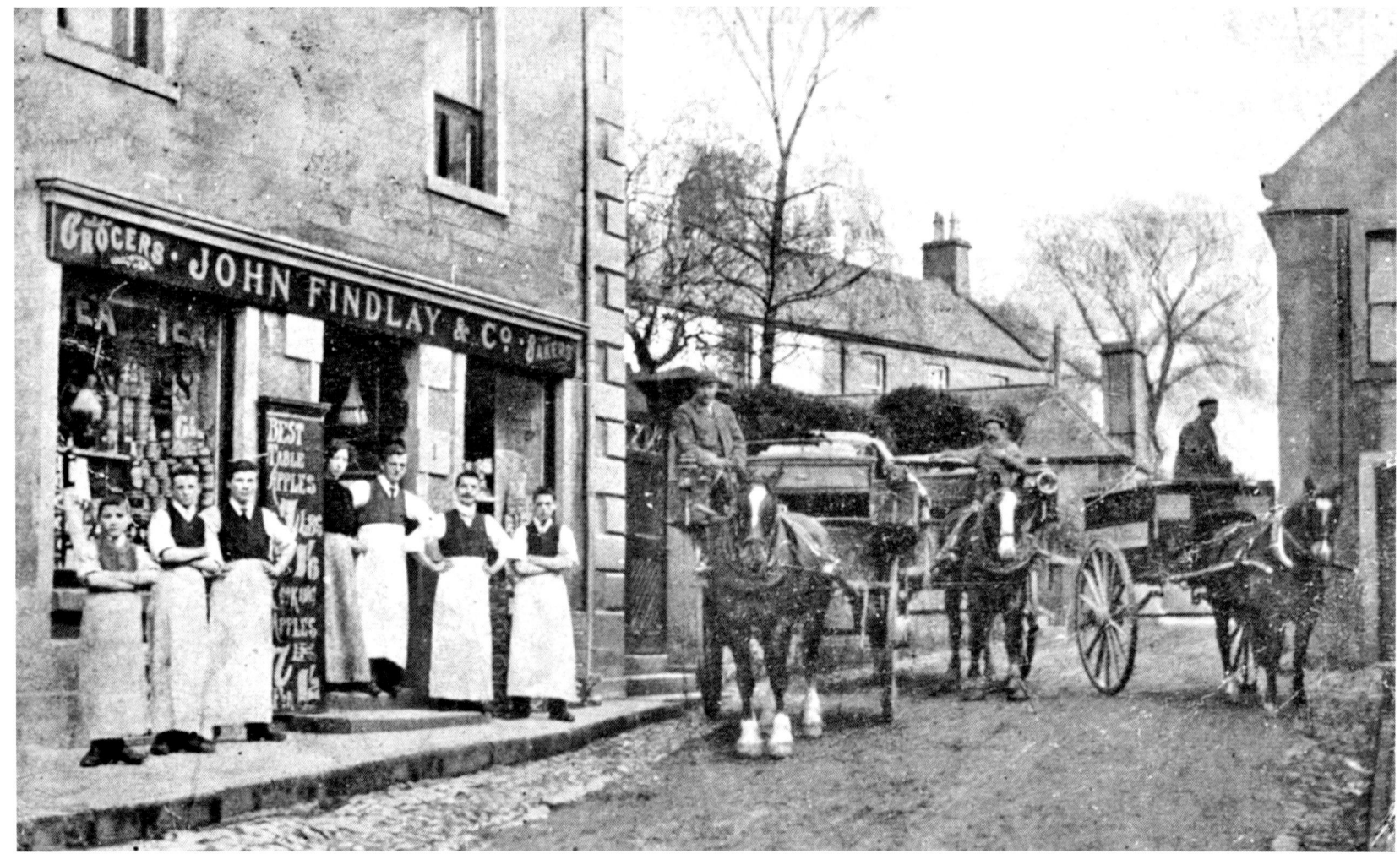

Dropping down into the town from the hills is Hill Street where John Findlay's grocery and baker's shop, seen here about 1907, was located. It was actually one of three 'Findlay' shops in the town and the presence of horse-drawn vans in the picture is a clear indication that the produce was also taken out for sale or delivery across the hinterland. At one time this older, upper part of the town was its commercial heart. Before the establishment of shops like Findlay's this was the market place where people from the glens and surrounding countryside would buy and sell produce in the street. Findlay's shop has since closed and the building converted for domestic use.

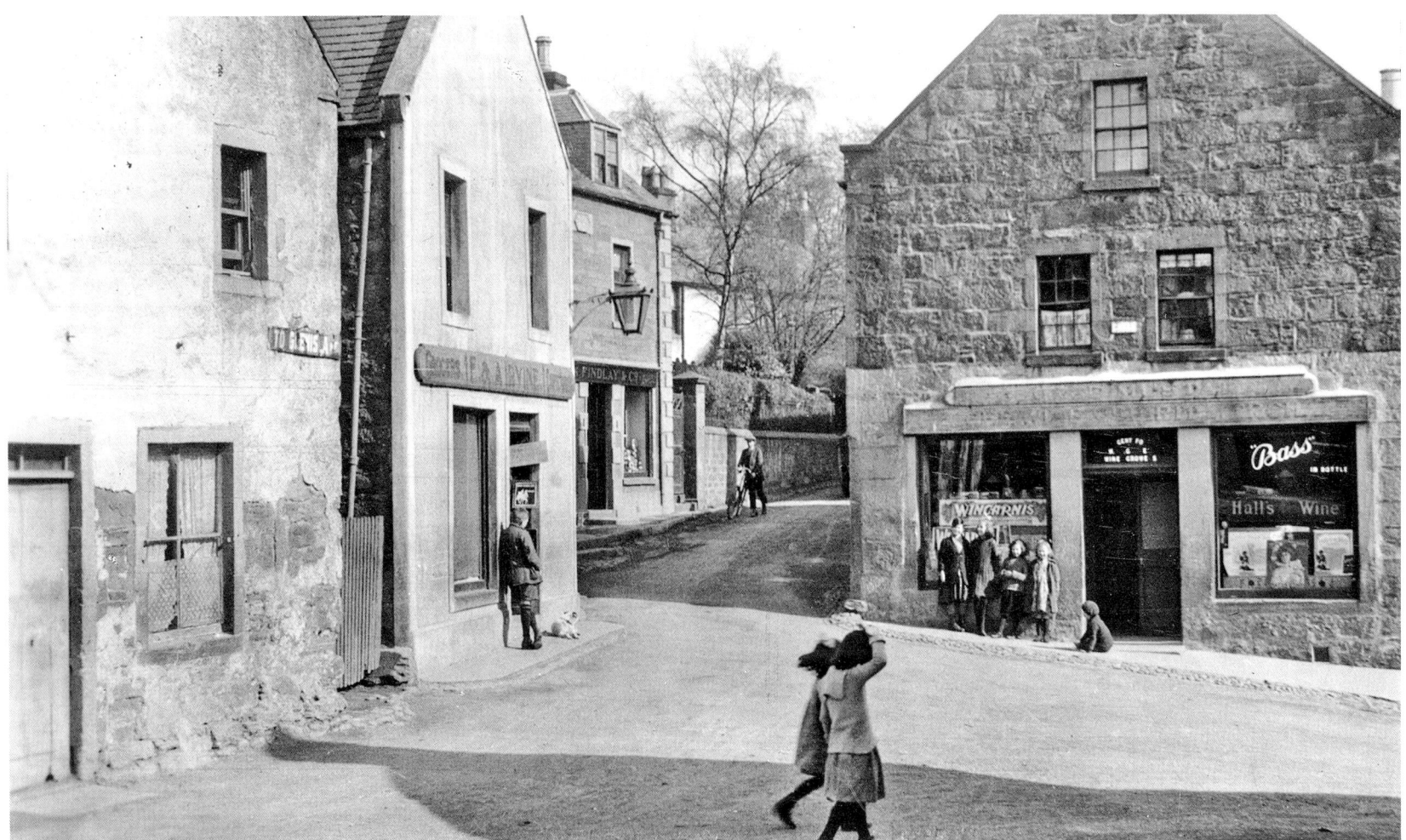

As a Burgh of Barony from 1488, Alyth was granted rights to hold fairs and markets. That status was given substance in 1670 when the then Earl of Airlie erected a market cross at the meeting point of the three main thoroughfares at the northern end of the town. It was a simple object, set on a stepped stone base as was customary at the time, but it acted as a focal point for traders to gather around. Later, shop buildings were located at the cross, as this early twentieth century picture looking toward Hill Street with Toutie Street on the right, shows. Facing camera is the licensed grocery of George Mustard and on the left E. & A. Irvine's grocery and confectionery business. There were other small businesses adjacent to the cross, but since then most of the buildings have gone, replaced by attractive gardens.

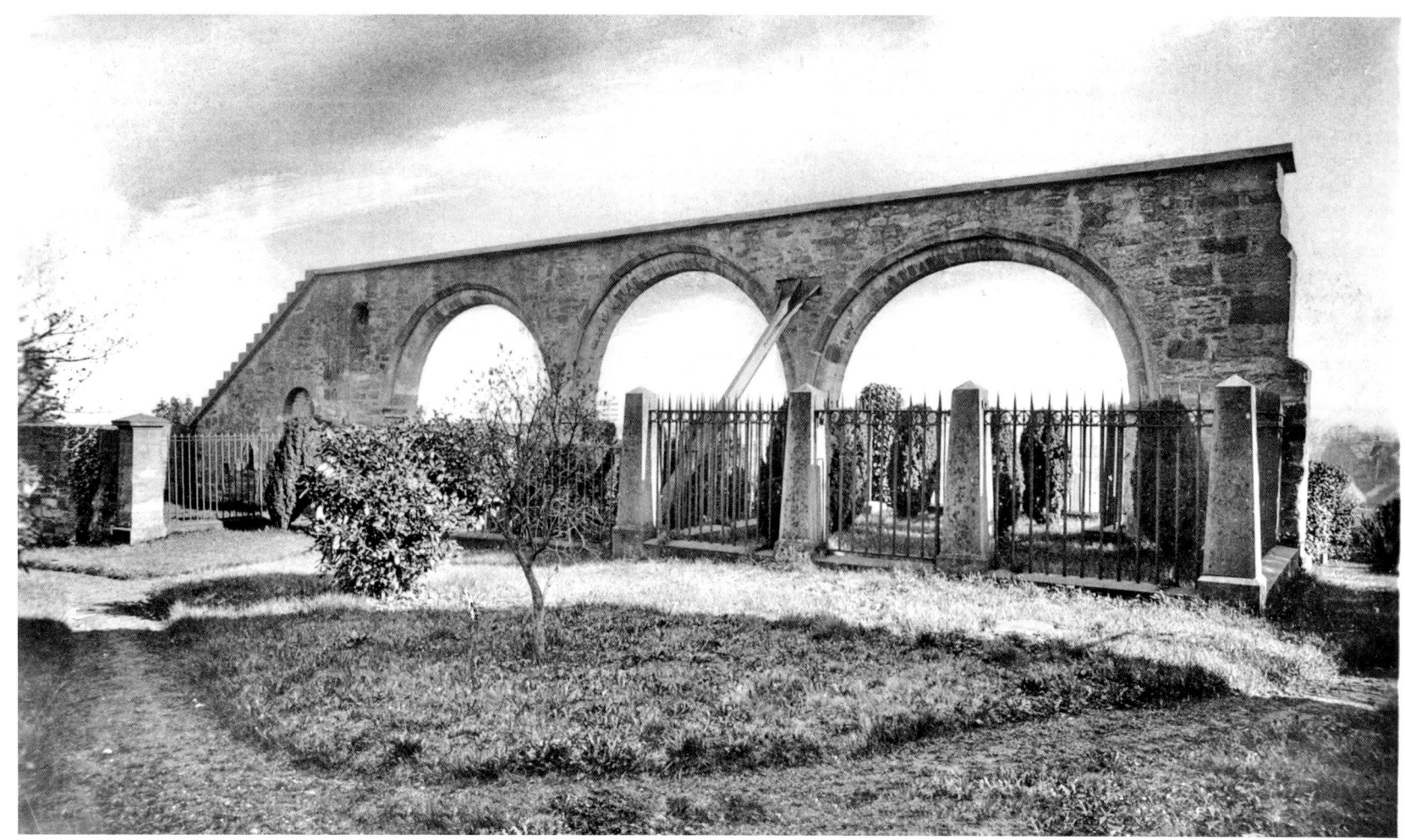

The older, upper part of Alyth is graced by another ancient structure, 'The Auld Arches'. These formed part of the parish church built on the site formerly occupied by a much earlier church dedicated to St Moluag, a contemporary of Saint Columba. After the Reformation of 1560, the church remained as the centre of religious worship for the parish until a new church was built in the 1830s. Abandoned, it soon became ruinous with only the north arcade that separated the nave from the north aisle remaining. Standing as a poignant ruin amongst the gravestones, the arches became a feature of historic interest for the town. Set in amongst the graves are some 'Pictish cross slabs' – large flat stones with a cross, carved or inscribed on the face by those early inhabitants of Scotland, the Picts. Carved on the face of a few more recent stones are the symbols of trades.

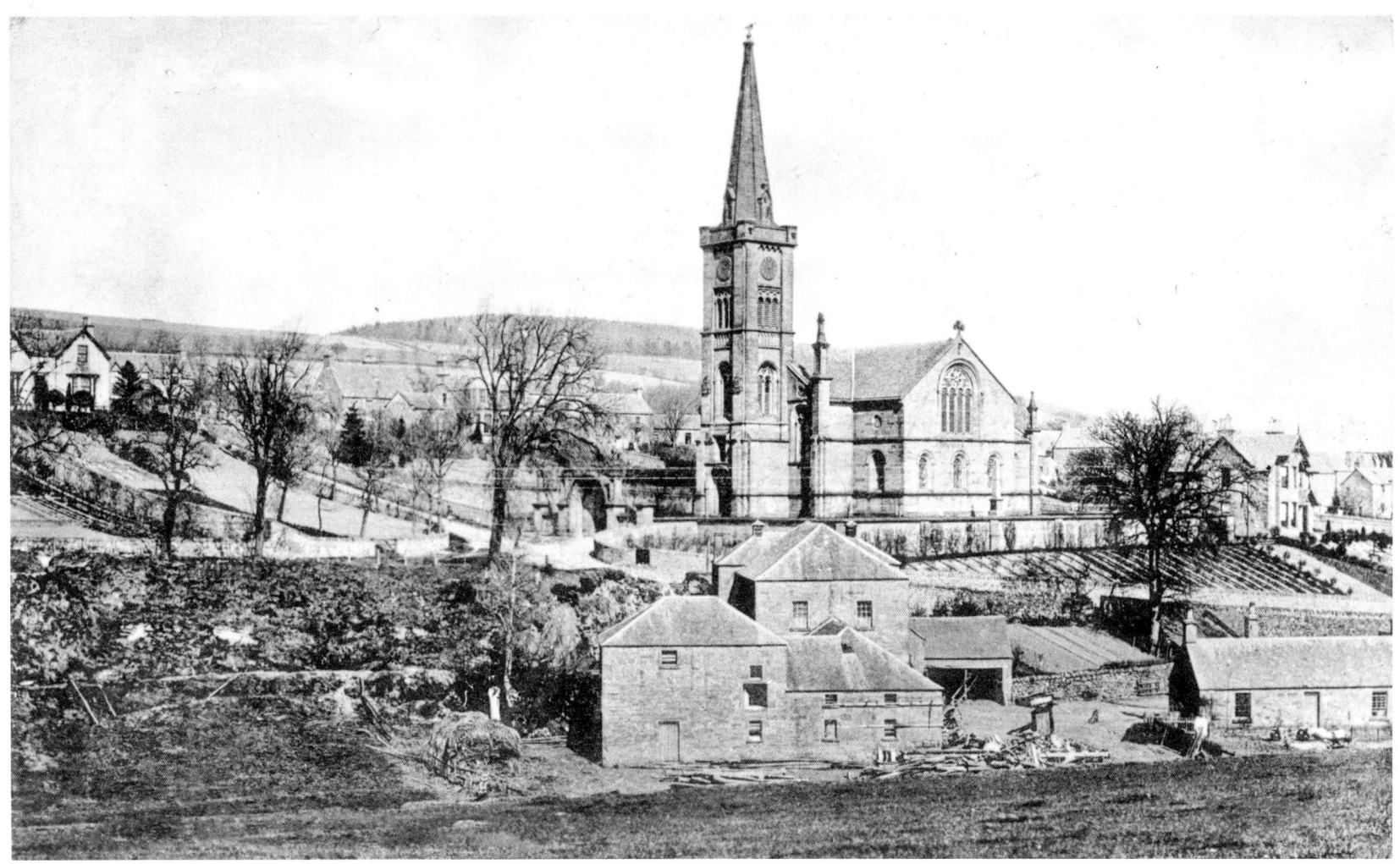

A new Alyth Parish Church situated on Kirk Brae, a couple of hundred yards to the west of the old church, was built between 1836 and 1839 to the designs of Edinburgh-based architect Thomas Hamilton. It is seen here commanding the high ground to the north of the town. Rising from this elevated site, the distinctively tall spire makes a splendid focal point. A Pictish cross slab, similar to those in the old churchyard and unearthed during construction of the manse in 1887, is displayed in the entrance porch. The church also contains some fine windows created by notable stained glass artists and a memorial, unveiled in October 1922, to the men of the parish who died during the First World War. The foreground mill indicates the closeness of the burn.

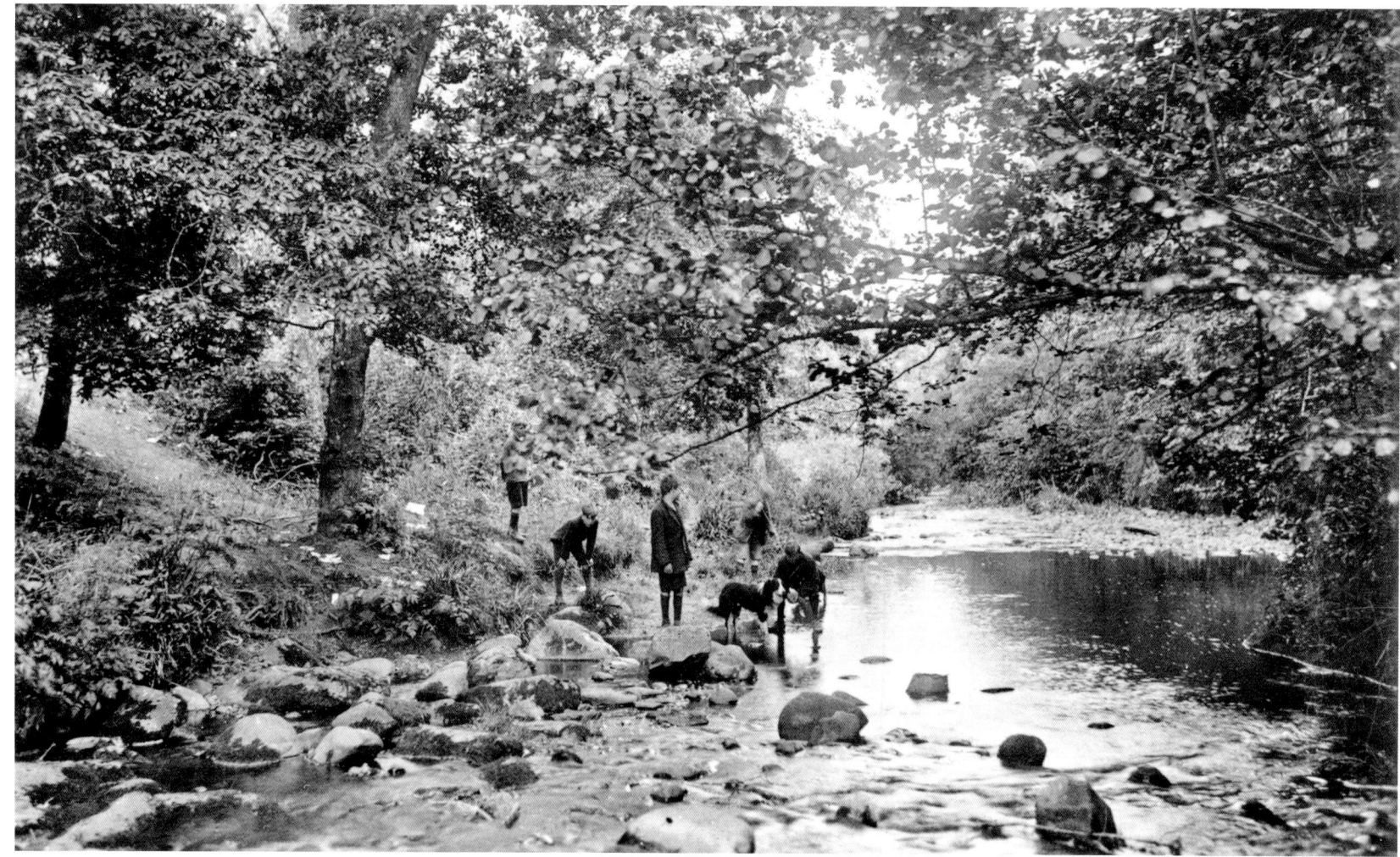

Tumbling down from the hills to the north and sweeping past Bamff House to the west, Alyth Burn flows on toward the town through the beautiful Den of Alyth. Had this scenic delight been situated further north and west, Gaelic speakers might have called it 'glen', but toward the east of Scotland such features are often named 'den' an early form of the Old English 'dene'. Whatever the name it would be wonderful. Carved over millennia through Old Red Sandstone, the Den is characterised by high cliff-like sides and a bubbling burn strewn with boulders. Deeply wooded with a variety of trees and wildflowers, and an abundance of wildlife, the den has been declared a Site of Special Scientific Interest (SSSI) – it is certainly special.

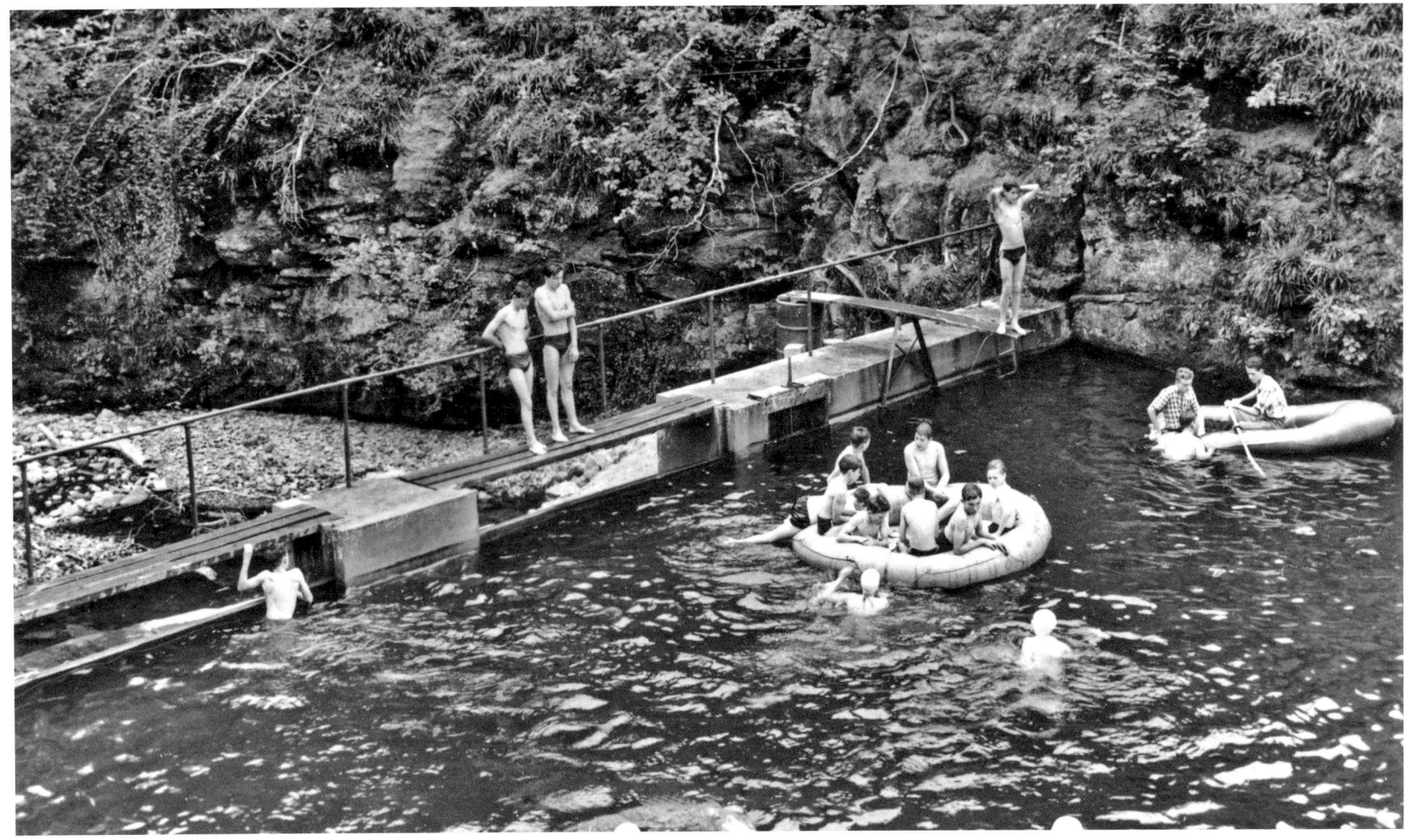

The Den has always been important to Alyth. Much of the stone used to construct buildings in the town came from a quarry at its lower end, and dams and weirs across the burn channelled water to mills, but appreciation of its value has changed over the years. Gifted to the town in 1923 by local landowners, the Earl of Airlie and A. G. Kinloch-Smyth of Balhary to make it more accessible, brushwood was cleared, paths laid, fences put up and bridges erected. Some folk used it as a peaceful retreat, others a playground as this picture of the swimming pool from the late 1950s shows. Created using voluntary effort it was evidently enjoyed by youngsters, happy to brave chilly water in those post-war austerity years. Since then, as people's appreciation of the environment has changed, the Den has become a scenic attraction for townspeople and visitors alike, and the disused quarry a car park.

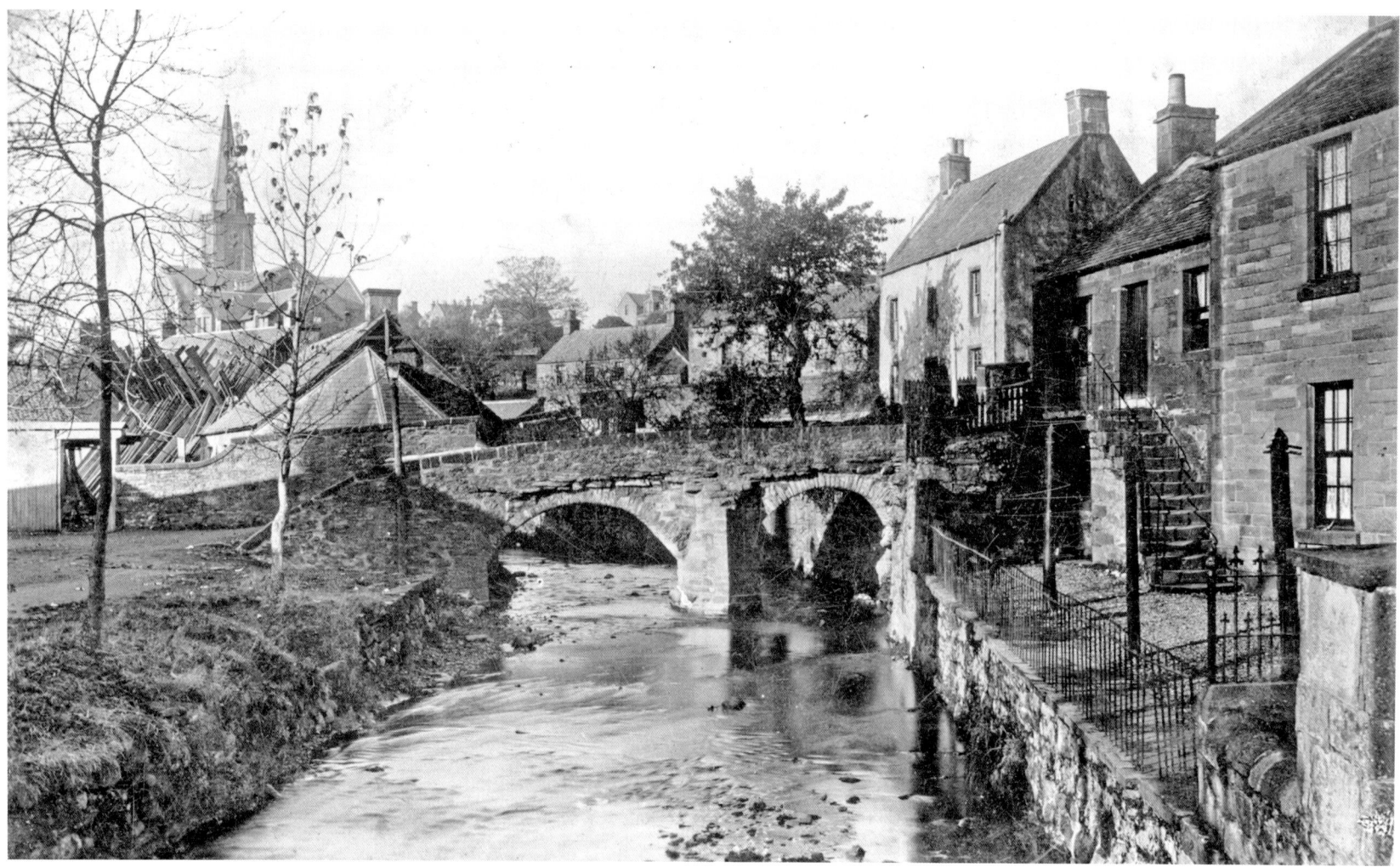

As it heads into the town the burn turns through ninety degrees and passes under one of Alyth's most attractive features, the 'Auld Brig'. The bridge is certainly old, although its actual age is uncertain. It appears to have been in existence by 1674 although late fifteenth and early sixteenth century dates have also been suggested. It was originally used by packhorses and because these tough creatures were laden with bulky panniers the bridge had no parapets as these could have impeded their progress. Parapets were added early in the nineteenth century when packhorses were no longer used. Bridge House, the distinctive two-storeyed building adjacent to the bridge, dates from 1728.

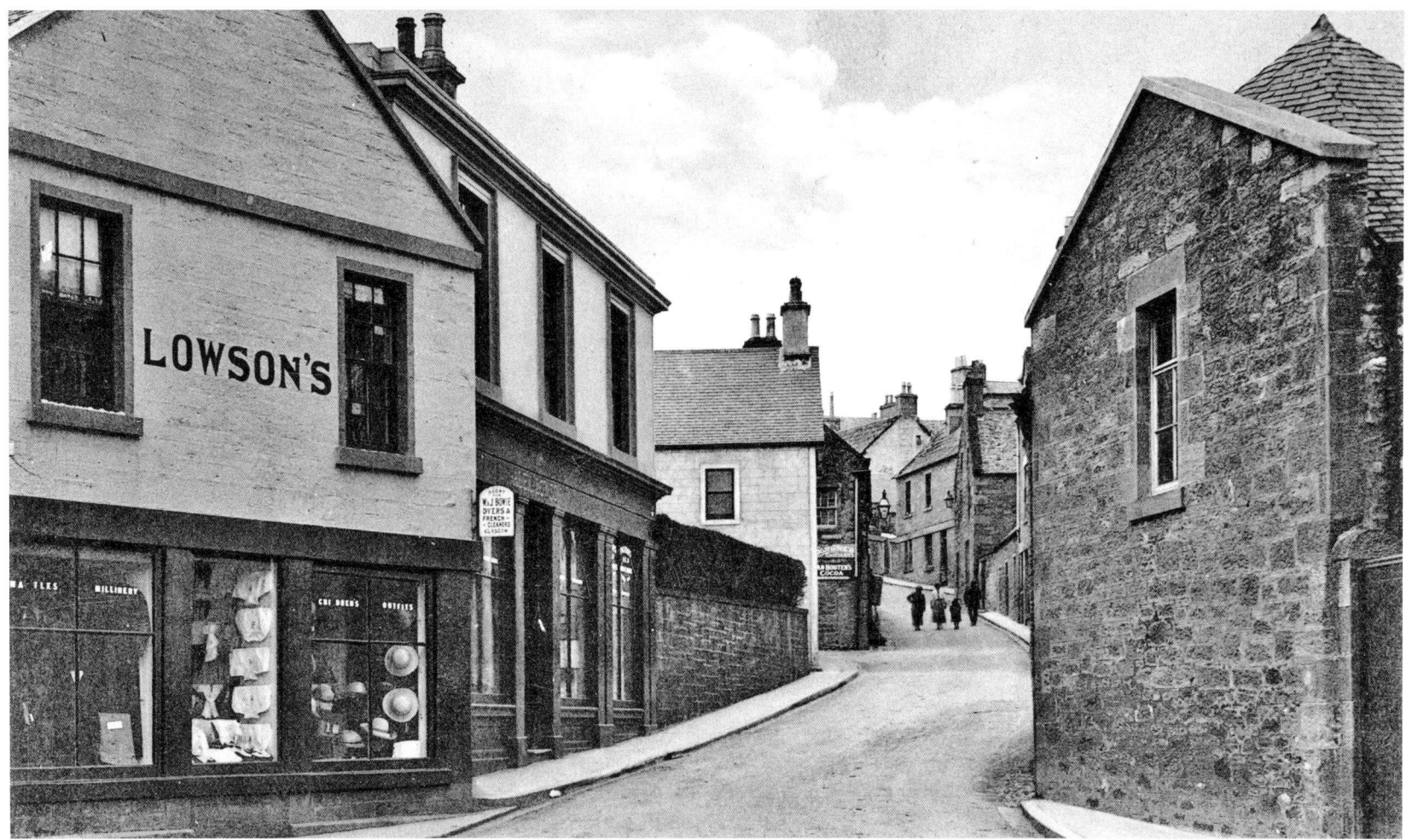

Toutie Street, seen here winding away from camera, is the link between the newer town, laid out alongside the burn and the old, upper town at the top of the hill. It was also, according to the popular definition of the name, the route taken by the herdsman who escorted cattle and sheep belonging to local people to and from the common grazing on Alyth Hill. He gathered the animals with a toot, tout, toutie on his horn and announced their return in a similar way. Such activity had long since passed into history by the time Alex Lowson had established his drapery shop at the foot of the street. The business sold a wide range of clothing including ladies costumes, gentlemen's suits, coats, millinery and furs. It also, perhaps surprisingly to modern perceptions, dealt in floor coverings, travelling rugs, bedding, and furniture.

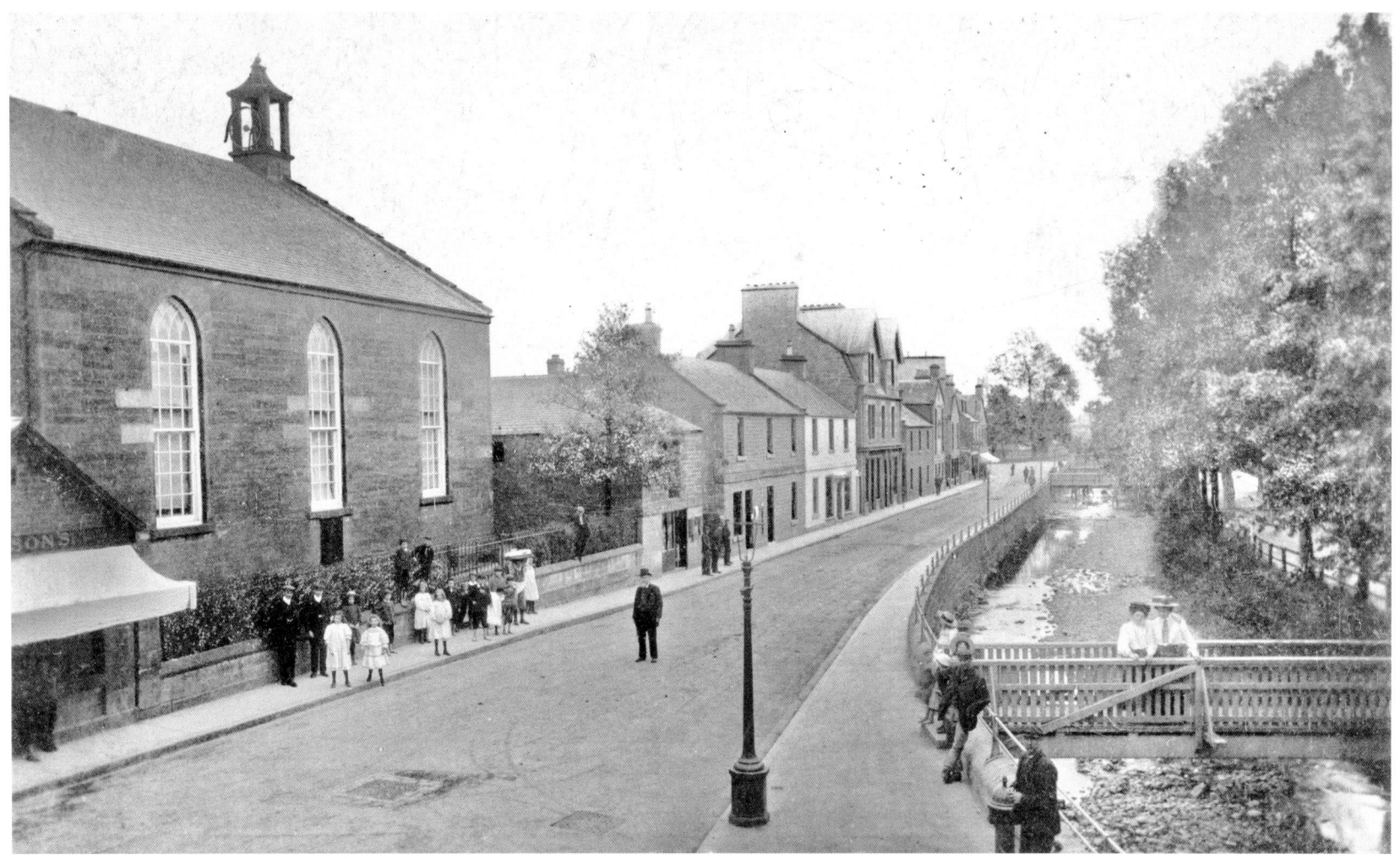

Heading south through the town, the burn is contained, or canalised, between built-up stone banks as this picture from about 1910 shows. On the left, the prominent building with a birdcage bellcote is the Barony Church built in the aftermath of the Disruption of 1843 when the Free Church broke away from the established Church of Scotland. For over a hundred years schisms and disputes had been chipping away at church unity, but the Disruption was a major event that caused widespread social upheaval and a proliferation of new church buildings. And then, in 1929, the churches largely reunited and new uses had to be found for many of the buildings erected in the heat of dispute. The Barony Church has since become a visitor centre and café.

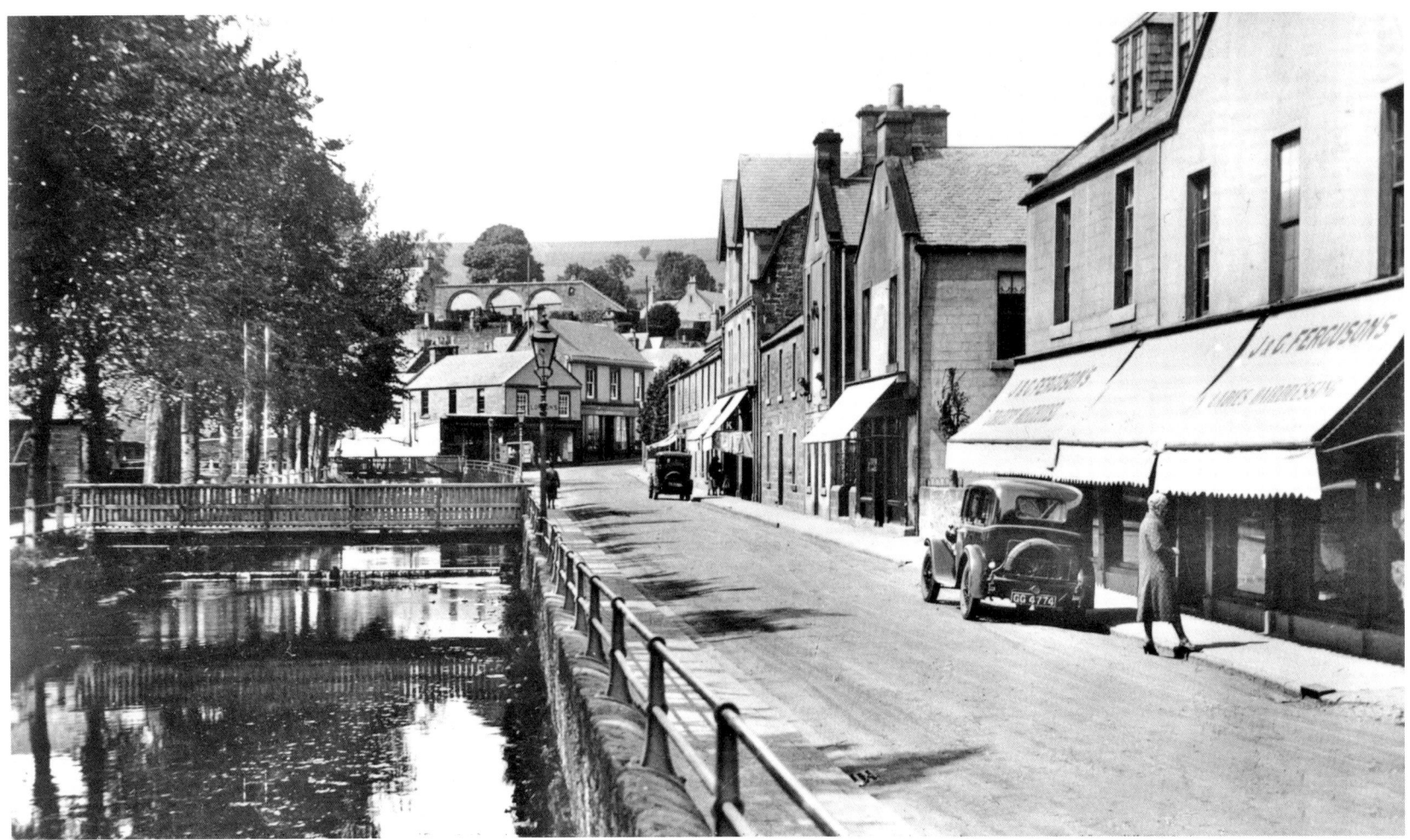

Another building that aims to welcome visitors is Alyth Museum, on the left of this picture looking north up Commercial Street about 1930. Formerly housing a collection of local history interest it has since been adapted as the hub of the outdoor Cateran Ecomuseum: Caterans were marauding cattle raiders and robbers whose reputation for badness seems to have been given a makeover to meet the demands of modern tourism. Facing the canalised burn, the buildings of Commercial Street enjoy a pleasant outlook and the many shops give substance to the appropriateness of the street name. In the foreground, Ferguson's shop was a drapery that, like Lowson's, which can be seen at the top of the street, sold a full range of ladies and gents clothing, fancy goods and floor coverings. It also offered, as is clear from the awning, a ladies hairdressing service.

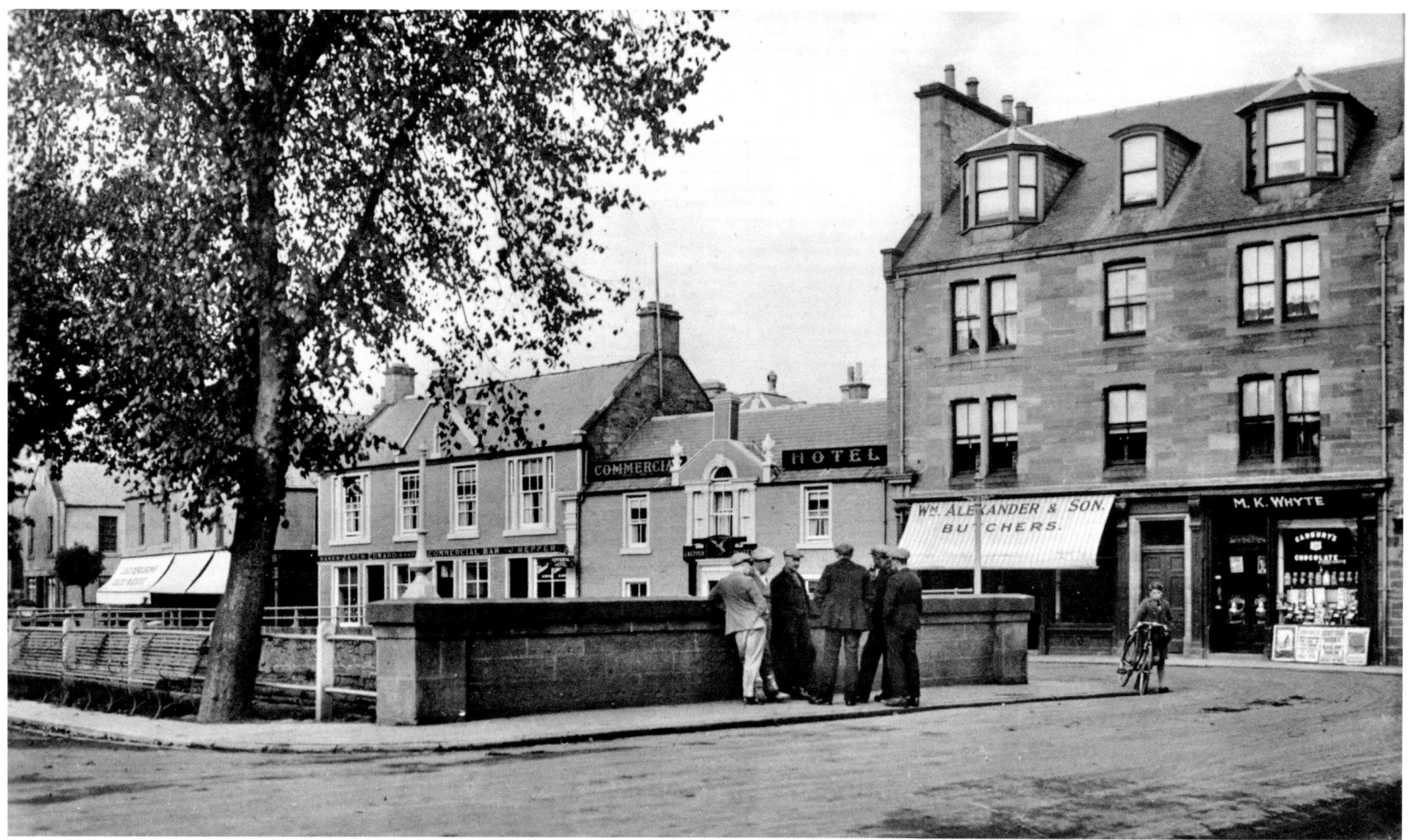

One of the most significant buildings on Commercial Street was the Commercial Hotel seen here from Bridge Street. The building itself is unremarkable, but it was formerly the home of James Sandy who, despite infirmity, put nimble fingers and mental prowess to such effect that he has been called a creative or inventive genius. He made musical instruments, clocks, artificial limbs, false teeth and optical instruments. He also devised improvements to spinning machinery, so important for the textile industries in Alyth. But the invention he will be best known for was the so-called invisible hinge, which allowed wooden snuff boxes to remain air tight and thus keep the contents dry and in good condition. The 'Commercial' name has since been dropped in favour of the locally more apt Alyth Hotel.

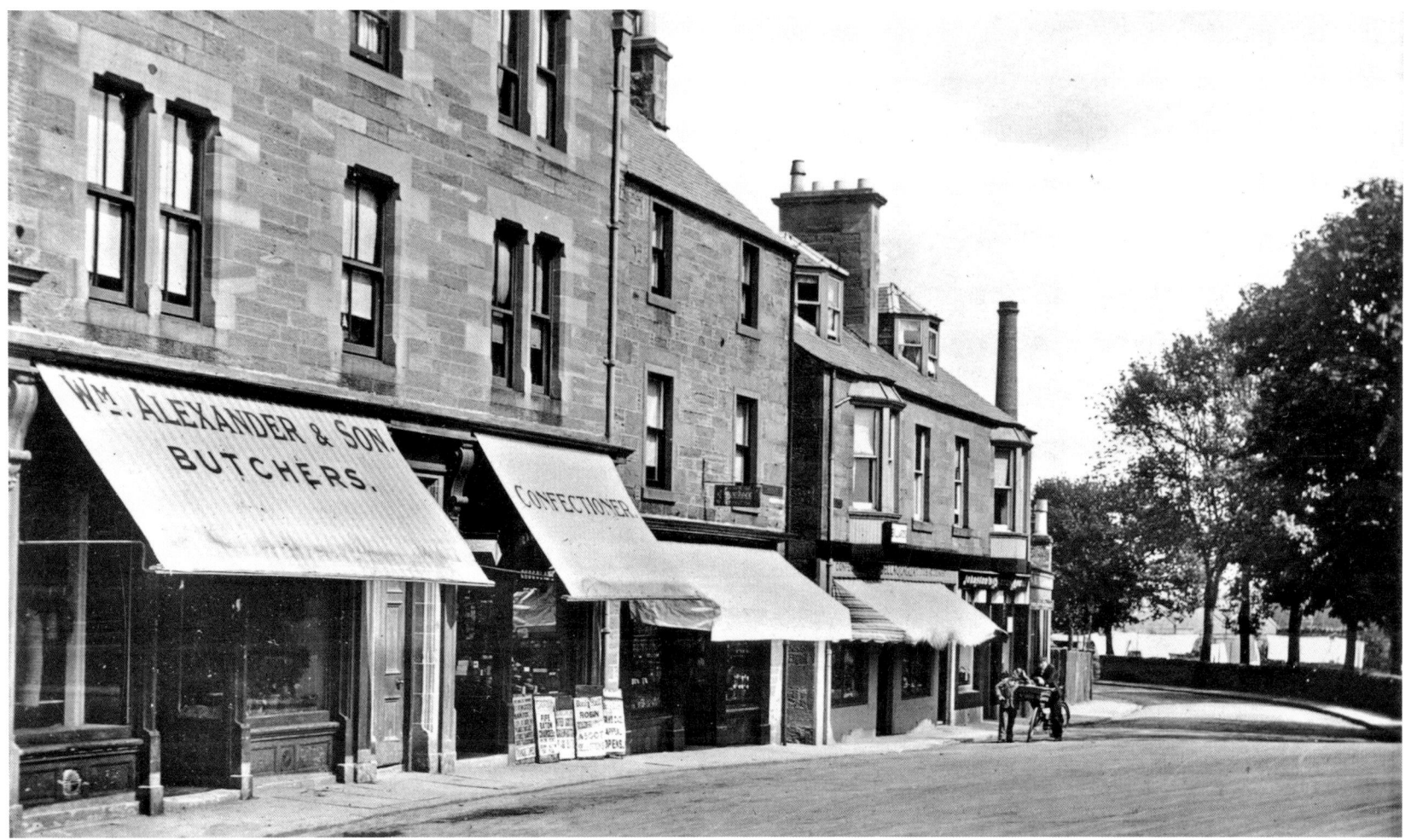

The southern end of Commercial Street is seen here in the early 1930s leading into Mill Street. It was the location of the woollen mill and also the Alyth Gas Light Company's works, which made fuel for street lighting and domestic use, and gave the town some scary moments. In December 1876 the roof of the retort house caught fire. People came to watch, but seeing the blaze get out of control and fearing an explosion many rushed home to turn off their meters. The mains were also shut down. The principal danger eased after the roof collapsed, but the town was without gas for a while. In another fire in March 1916 the manager Alexander Watt was burned and injured trying to unblock a gas pipe, but continued to direct proceedings when the Royal Engineers arrived to put out the fire. The gas industry was nationalised in 1948 before the discovery of North Sea gas led to the closure of town works.

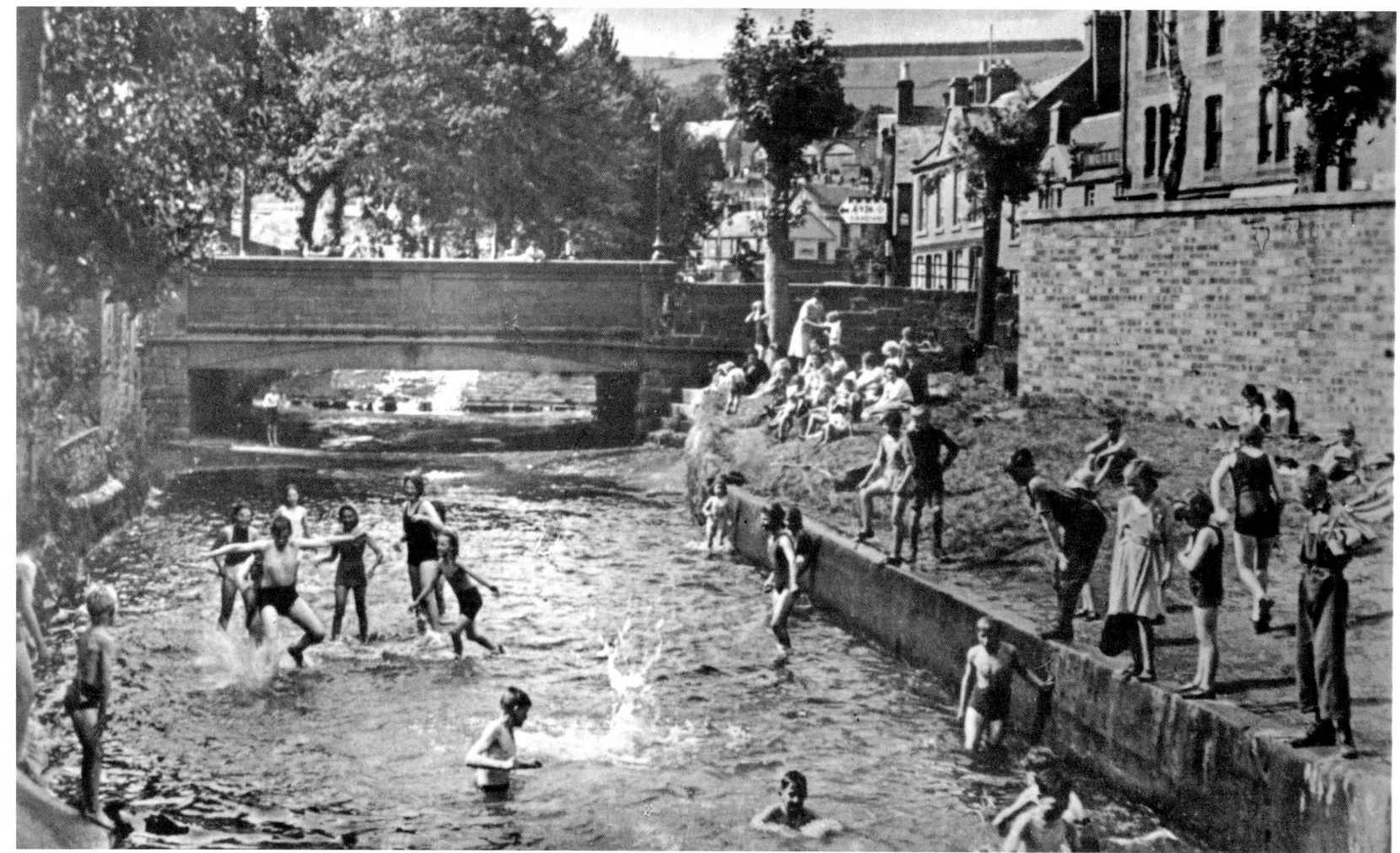

While older, more boisterous children could splash about in the swimming pool in the Den smaller children got happily wet in the paddling pool formed in the burn just to the south of the bridge between Commercial Street and Market Square. The picture gives a good indication of how popular the pool could be – it must have been a warm day. A play park of swings and things was also set up on the adjacent Burn Green turning this corner of Alyth into a children's paradise. The buildings of Commercial Street and Mill Street can be seen above the wall on the right. Such a scene shows the burn as a benign presence in the town, but that was not always so as the picture on the facing page shows.

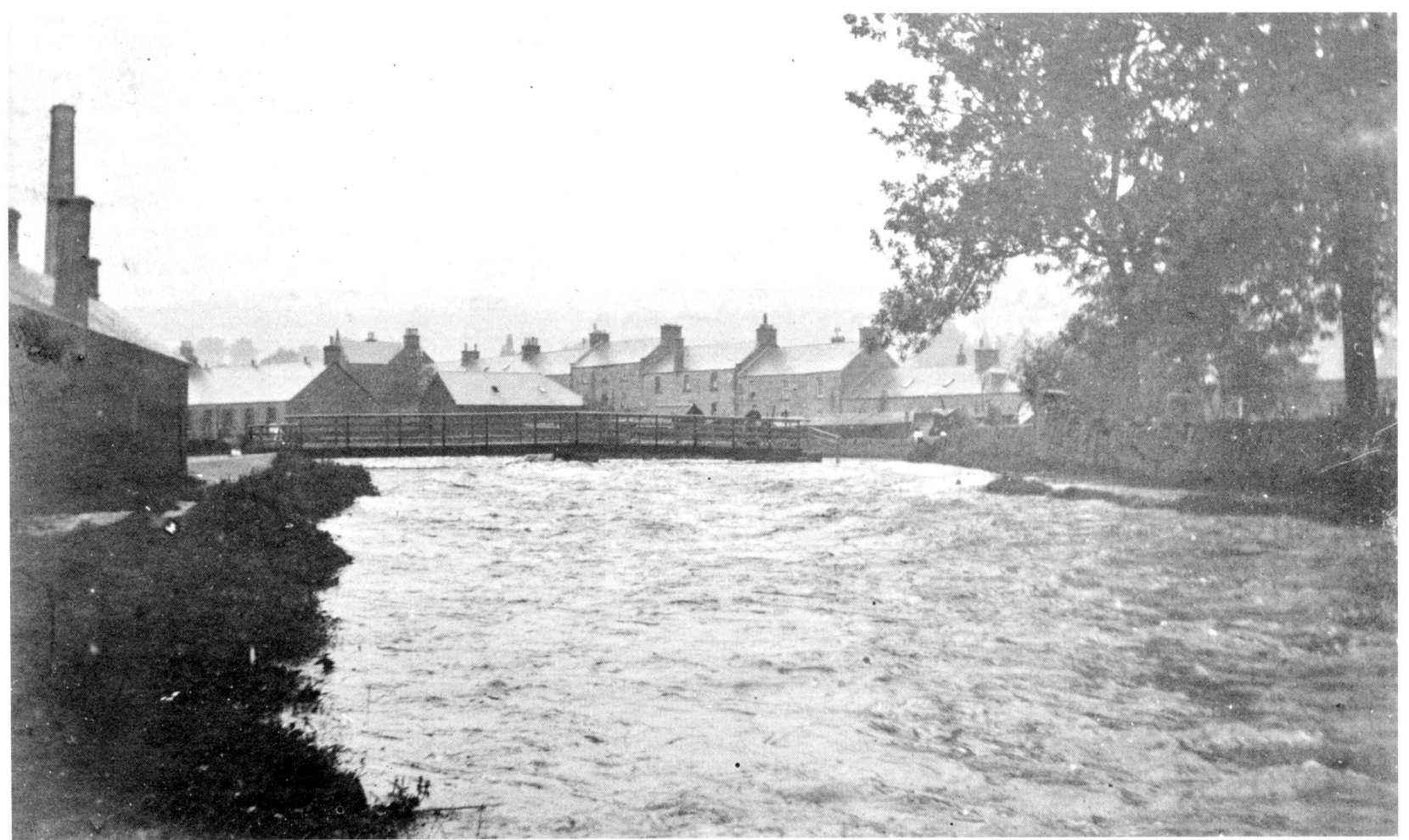

In late August and early September 1903 it rained, and it rained, and it rained. Indeed it rained for eight days causing great damage to crops and the worst flooding in the district for over twenty years. The Alyth Burn rose rapidly and swept through the town carrying away bridges at the wool mill and the quarry. Bridges in the town centre were in danger of a similar fate and so some men secured one with ropes and, presumably at some danger to themselves, relieved the pressure on others by guiding tree roots and debris away from them. As this picture shows, the water overtopped the banks threatening to inundate the Commercial Hotel and other properties adjacent to the burn, but there was at least one lighter moment when former Provost Tod captured a small trout in Commercial Street.

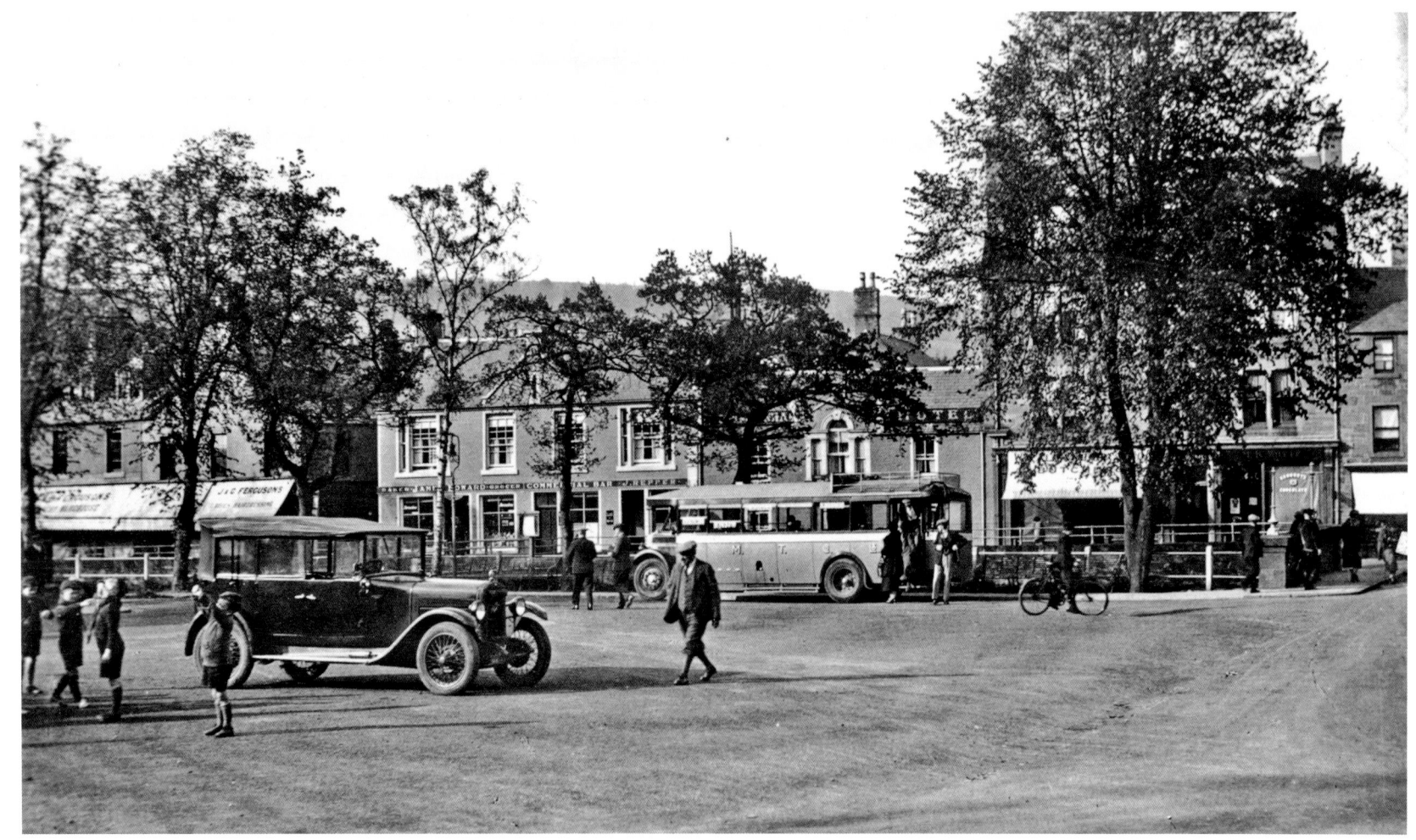

Over time, the centre of the town shifted across the burn to the west bank where the Market Square was created. It is seen here in 1932 with the buildings of Commercial Street in the background. A splendid civic space, it has evidently by this time become a place to park cars and an ideal town centre location for bus services. As the name implies, the Market Square was a place for business, duly acknowledged by the Bank of Scotland, which built its local branch on the north-east corner. In the adjacent building there was a newsagent and confectionery shop, and a hardware and crockery store originally operated by George Gordon and later by David Sim. The Square was also the location of a saddlers' business where many working horses had their harness made or repaired.

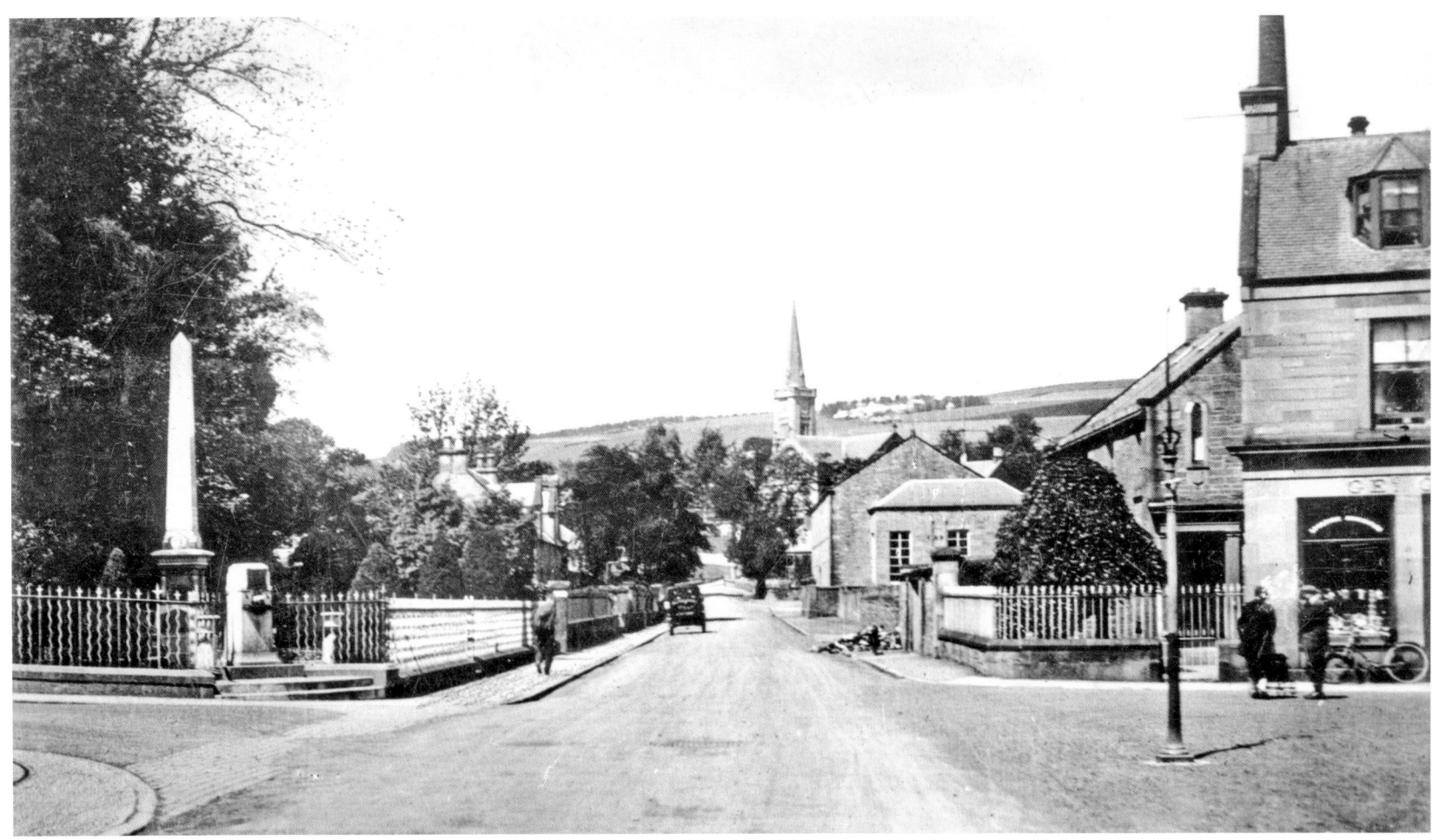

George Gordon's hardware shop is on the right hand edge of this picture looking north up Bamff Road from Market Square. On the left is the obelisk erected in 1901 to commemorate three local men who died in the South African or Boer War. Most prominent was the 9th Earl of Airlie, killed during the Battle of Diamond Hill in 1900. The loss of such a figure must have helped persuade the Town Council to mark his passing along with two other men, a lieutenant in the Black Watch killed in 1899 at Magersfontein and a Fife & Forfar Yeomanry trooper who died at sea. Prior to the war yeomanry regiments were intended only for home defence duties, but when the conflict went badly wrong for the regular army the men were called on to volunteer; many did and some did not come back. In that respect his death is significant because it presaged the call for volunteers when a much bigger conflict erupted in 1914.

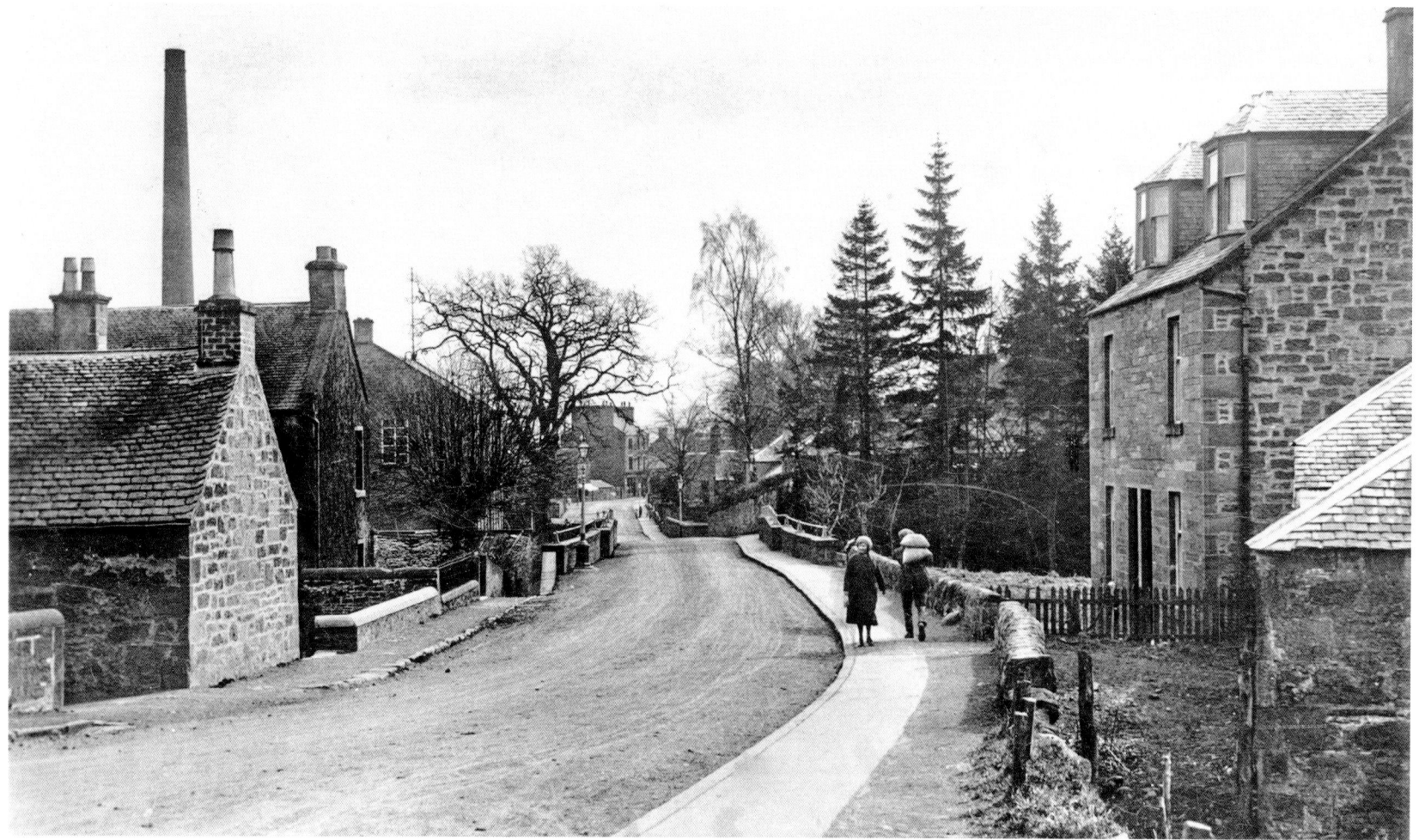

Bamff Road was another link with the old and new towns, but on the west side of the burn. It is seen here in the 1920s looking south from the Millhaugh. Just beyond the two pedestrians, the road narrows where it crosses the burn on a bridge situated upstream of the old packhorse bridge. There was a weir close to this Bamff Road Bridge that directed water to a plash mill where flax fibres were treated before being spun into linen yarn. That early facility developed into a major industry for the town, with a factory situated to the left of the picture, the tall chimney is a giveaway, but it is also an indicator that steam, not water became the principal source of power. Following a major fire in 1898 the business struggled and eventually ceased trading, with many people being thrown out of work or having to move elsewhere. The remaining buildings were later used by Forfar Carpets and for car restoration.

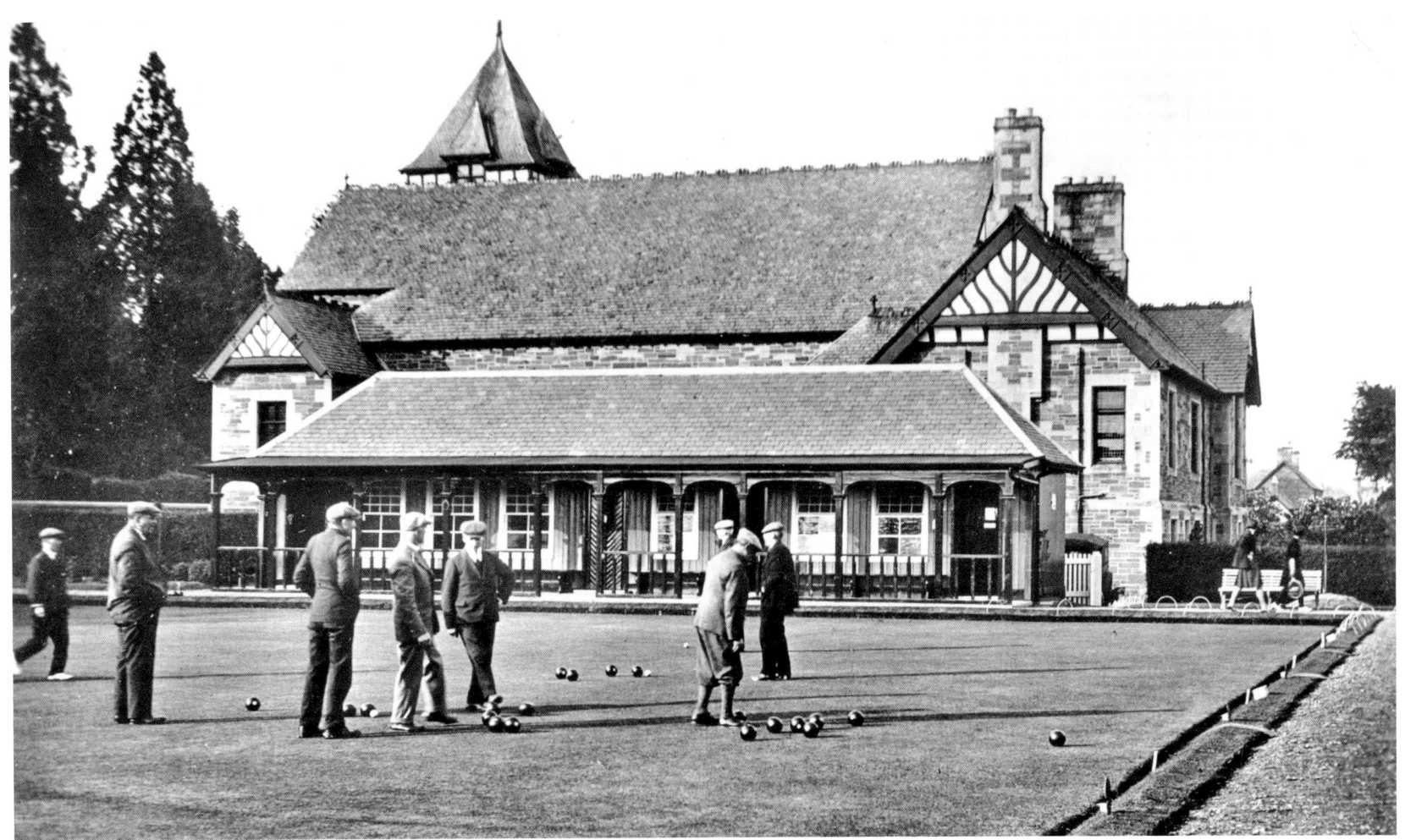

As befitted a proud community, Alyth got a new town hall in 1887. The architect, Andrew Heiton, was noted for his work on large country houses and some features like the half-timbered gable heads and tower, would not have looked out of place in such places. It was built on Albert Road, which intersects with Market Square beside the South African War Memorial, so was well connected and became a social centre where local groups held a variety of community gatherings like dances, or organised bazaars to raise funds for civic amenities. When movies became a popular form of entertainment, the hall gained another role as the town's cinema. Outdoor facilities were also developed alongside the hall, including two tennis courts and, as this picture from the early 1930s shows, the bowling green.

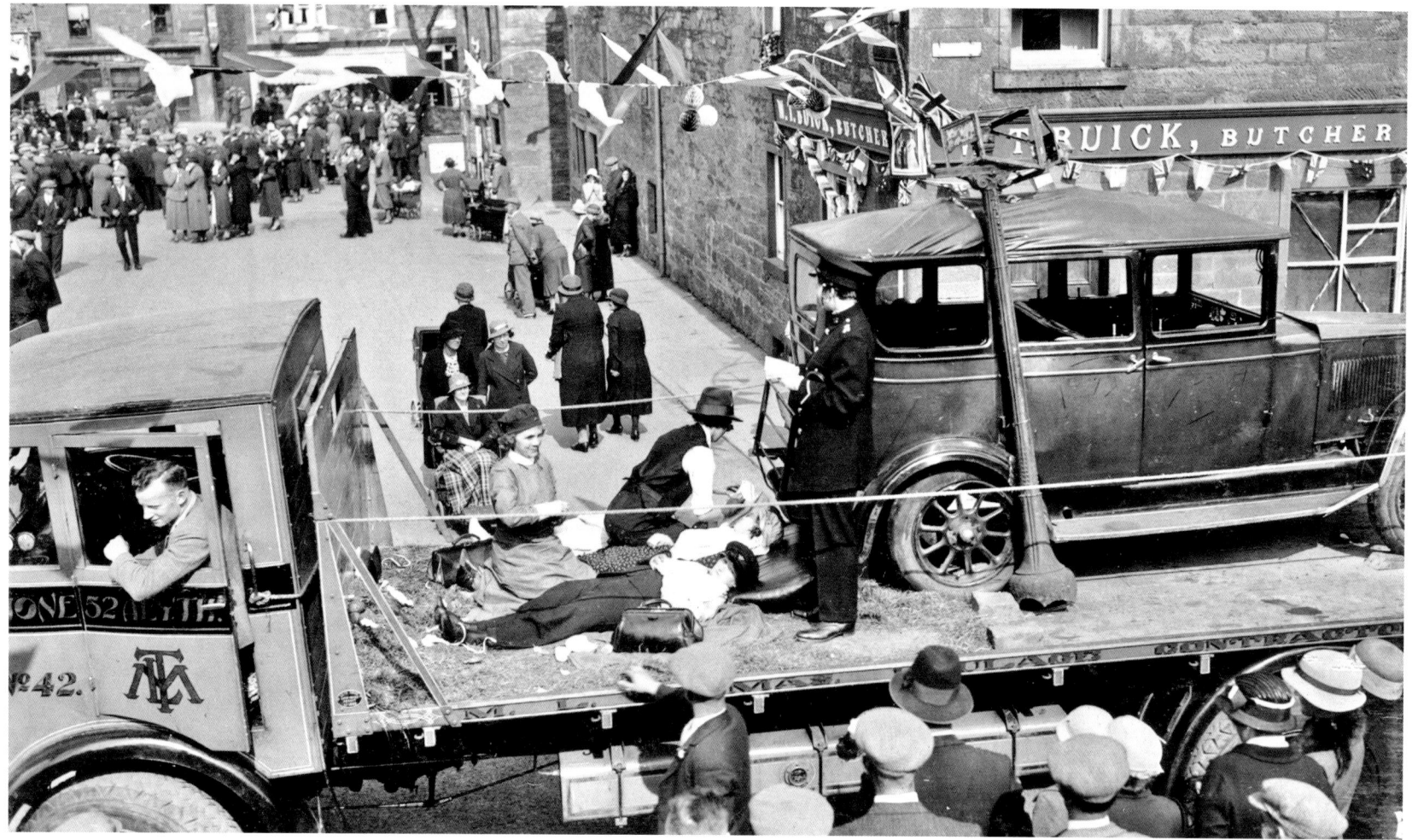

Market Square is in the background of this scene, which appears to show a dreadful road traffic accident. A lamppost has been broken, a car dented and a casualty is receiving attention. It is of course all a bit of theatre presented on the back of a lorry belonging to local haulage contractor Murray Thomas. He had made a number of vehicles available as floats on which various community groups were able to stage tableaux as part of the celebrations for King George V's Silver Jubilee in 1935. The wonderfully decorated floats included representations of Britannia, Canada, Cowboys and Indians, a wedding party, Meg Merrilees and her Gipsy Band from Sir Walter Scott's *Guy Mannering*, The Mad Hatter's Tea Party from *Alice in Wonderland* and many other themes. 'Road safety' appears to have been the subject of this float.

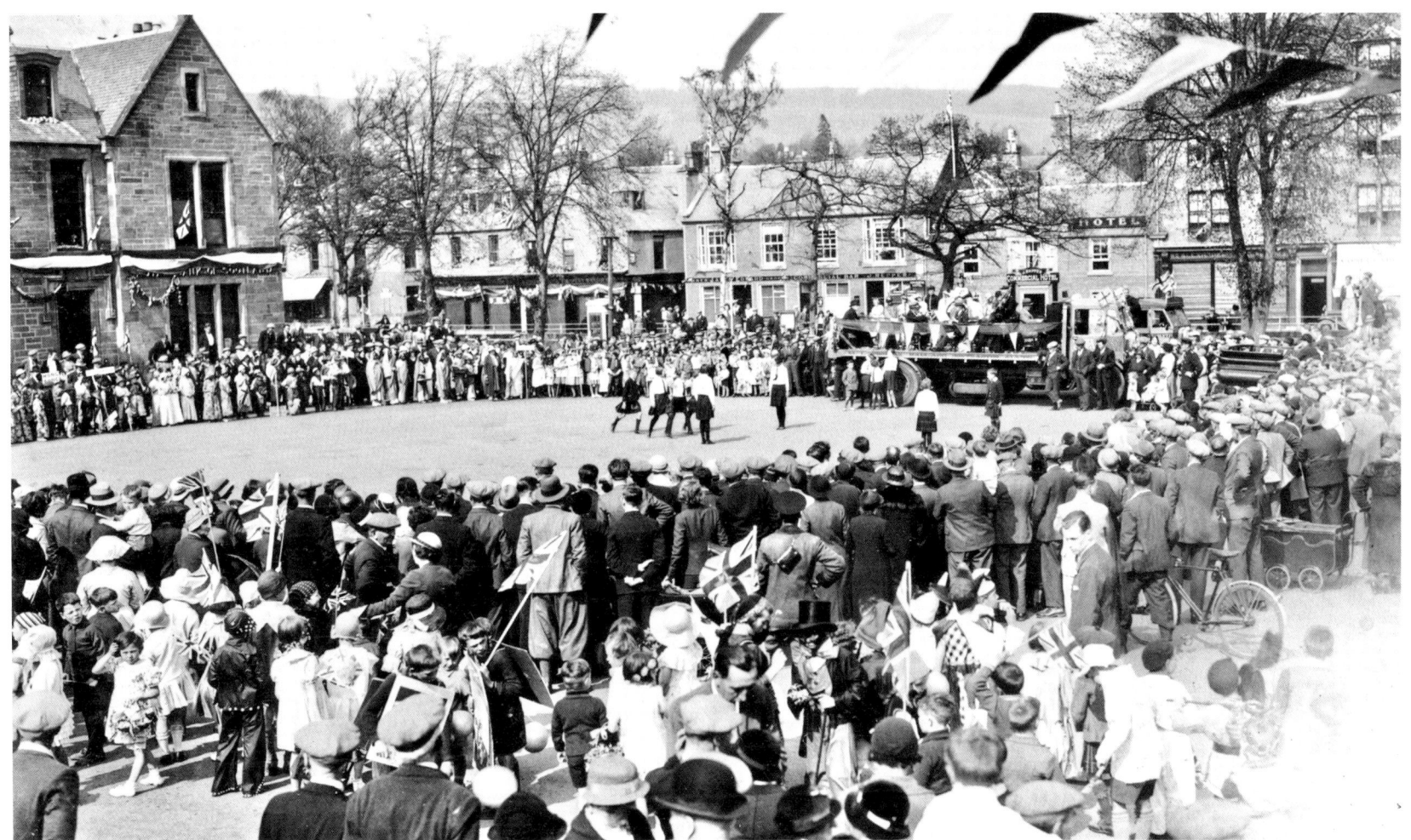

The floats were followed by a procession of children dressed to represent Scotland, England, Ireland and Wales, and the countries of East and West Africa, Australia, Canada, New Zealand, India, Burma, Hong Kong, and the West Indies. Others were dressed as heralds, fairies, flower girls, nurses, highlanders or miners, all part of the huge community effort that must have gone into making this a day to remember for the town. Crowds of people watched the parade and gathered at Market Square where there was country dancing to the music of Mr John Reid's Newtyle Orchestra. Children were later entertained by a film show and at the end of the day the Boy Scouts lit a bonfire on Alyth Hill. Two years later, the community did it all again with festivities to mark the Coronation of King George VI.

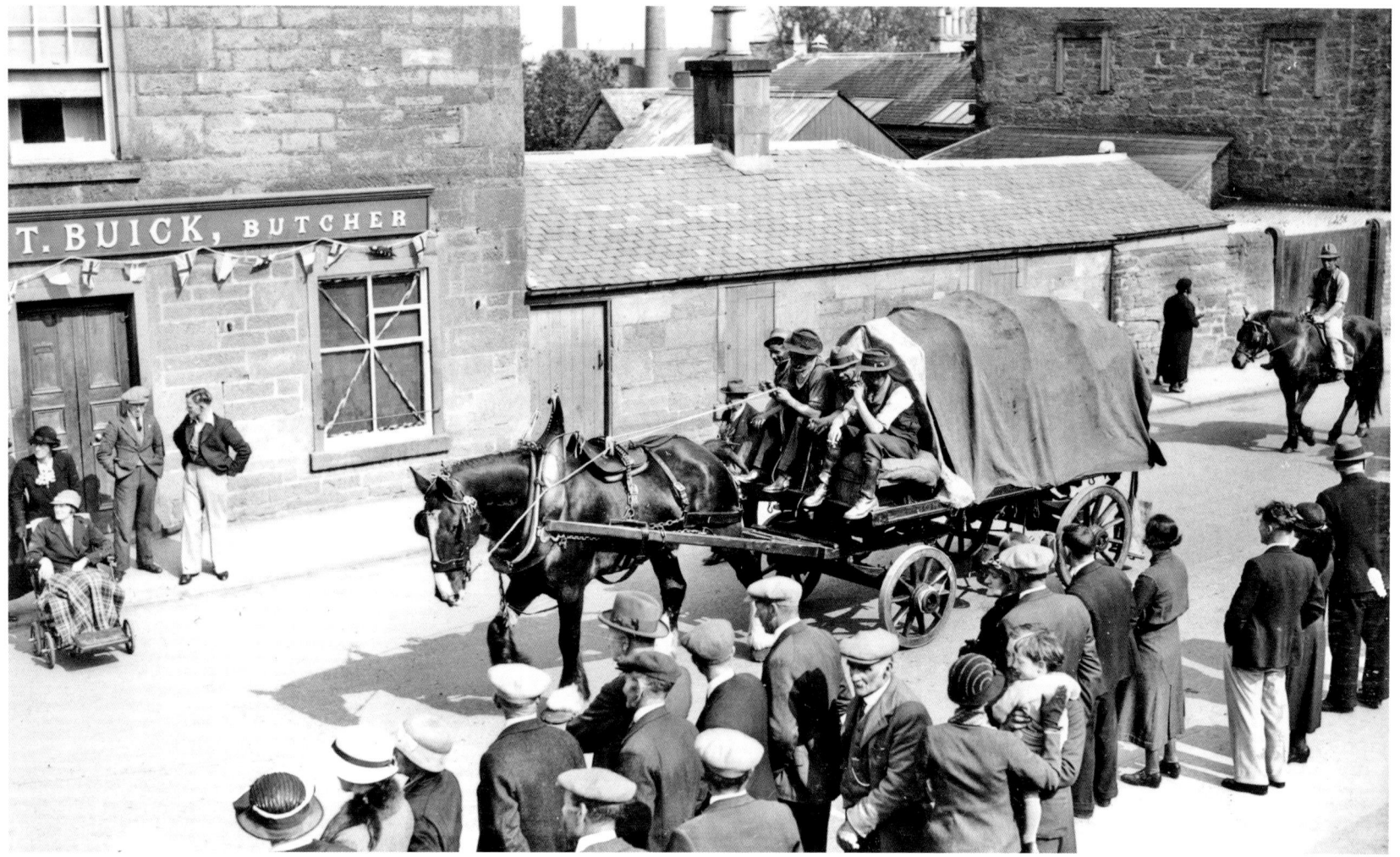

The Wild West came to town when this covered wagon took part in the Silver Jubilee parade of 1935. It is seen here passing the shop on the corner of Market Square and Airlie Street (actual address, No.1 Airlie Street), which butcher Walter T. Buick had taken over a few years earlier. The shop had a history of being used by butchers, or fleshers as they were formerly known, with the previous occupant, a Mr Cruickshank, promoting his business as a 'purveyor of the primest home-killed beef, mutton and lamb' (author's note: not sure if primest is a word, but it does convey an unambiguous message). Customers were also invited to try pickled tongue, corned beef, and salt rounds. There was another butcher's shop further down Airlie Street.

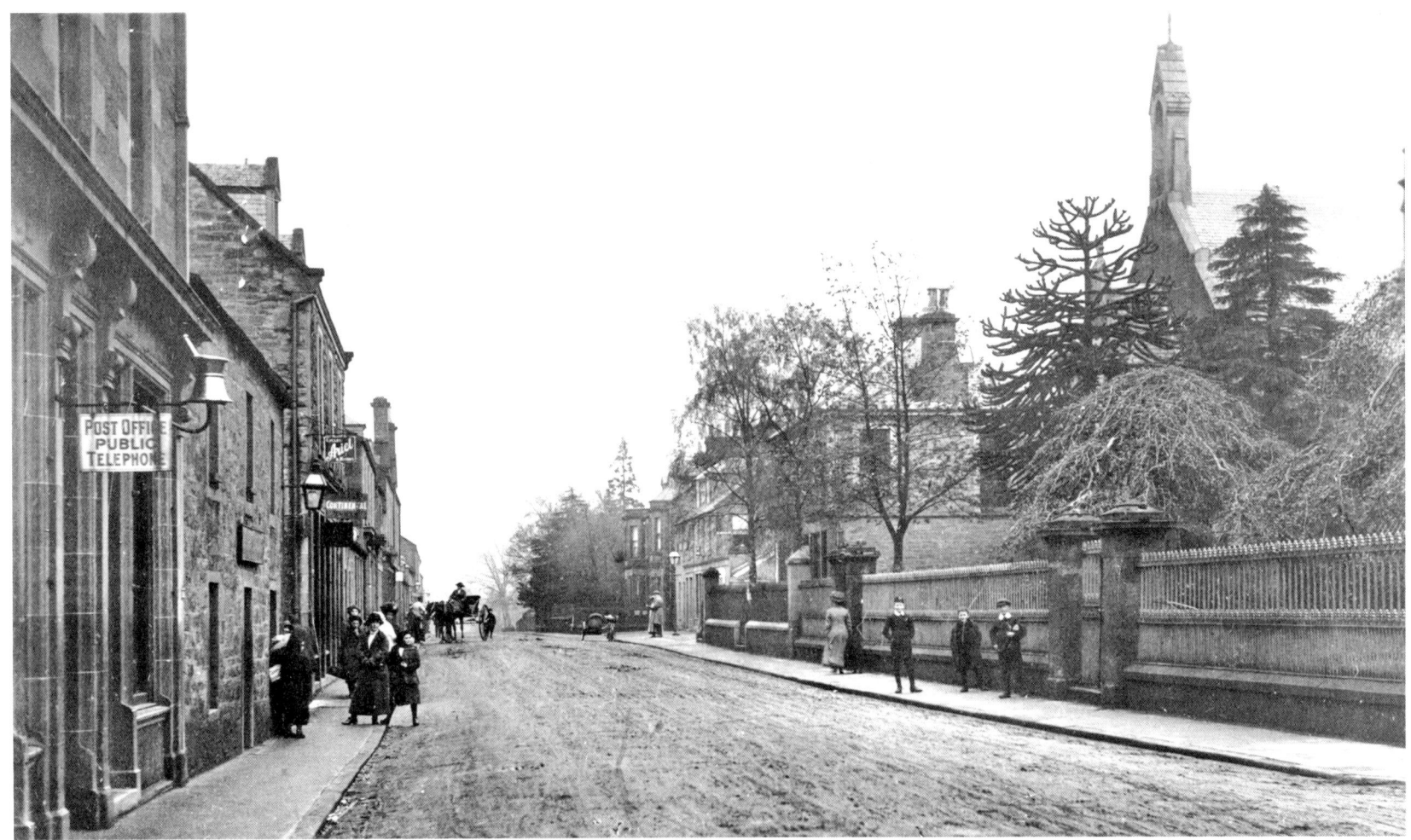

Unlike the old town streets, which undulated and rambled according to the lie of the land, Airlie Street ran straight and true, with neighbouring nineteenth century streets laid out on a grid pattern as seen here looking south about 1914 with the Post Office, which had formerly been situated at the Cross, on the left. A sign, that is also a 'sign of the times', advises people that a telephone was available for public use, a facility rendered just about obsolete in the modern world by the ubiquitous mobile 'phone. The mortar and pestle sign indicates a chemist's shop next door. The building with a tall bellcote on the opposite side of the street was initially used by adherents of the United Presbyterian Church, which had been formed in 1847 as an amalgam of dissenting churches that had proliferated in Scotland in the preceding century. Following wider church reunification it became the Parish Church hall.

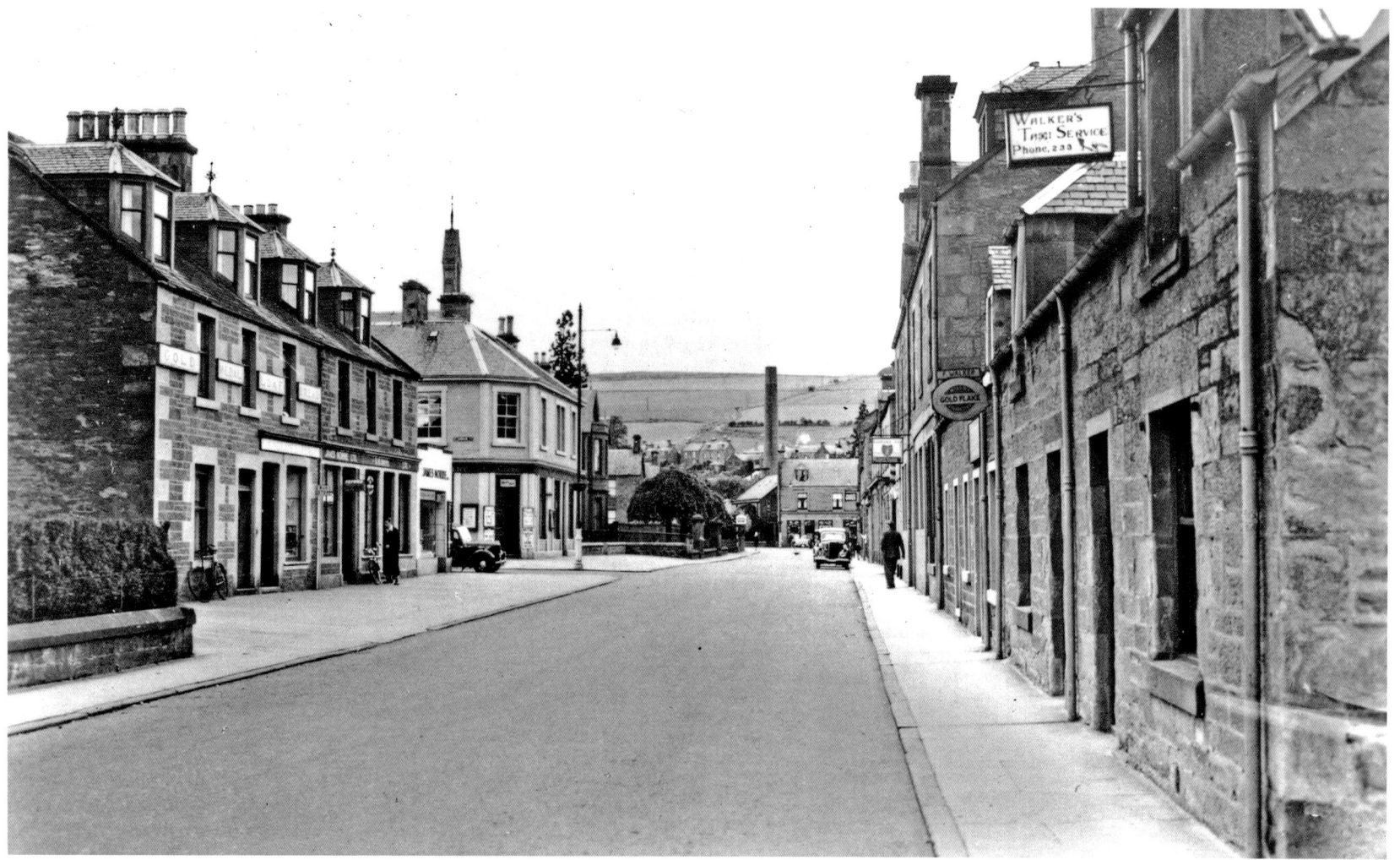

Airlie Street is seen looking north in this 1950s view when not many people owned a motor vehicle and traffic volumes were evidently low, a state of affairs that Walker's Taxi Service, whose sign can be seen on the right, probably welcomed. The junction with St Andrew Street is on the left with a single-storey pale-coloured building on the corner. This was the shop of James Norrie Ltd. printers and publishers who produced the *Alyth Gazette and Guardian*, and guidebooks to the town. A stationer and tobacconist, the shop stocked a range of gifts, postcards, books and fancy goods, and dealt in sports goods like golf balls, tennis rackets and balls. The business also sold cameras and film, and provided a photographic developing and printing service.

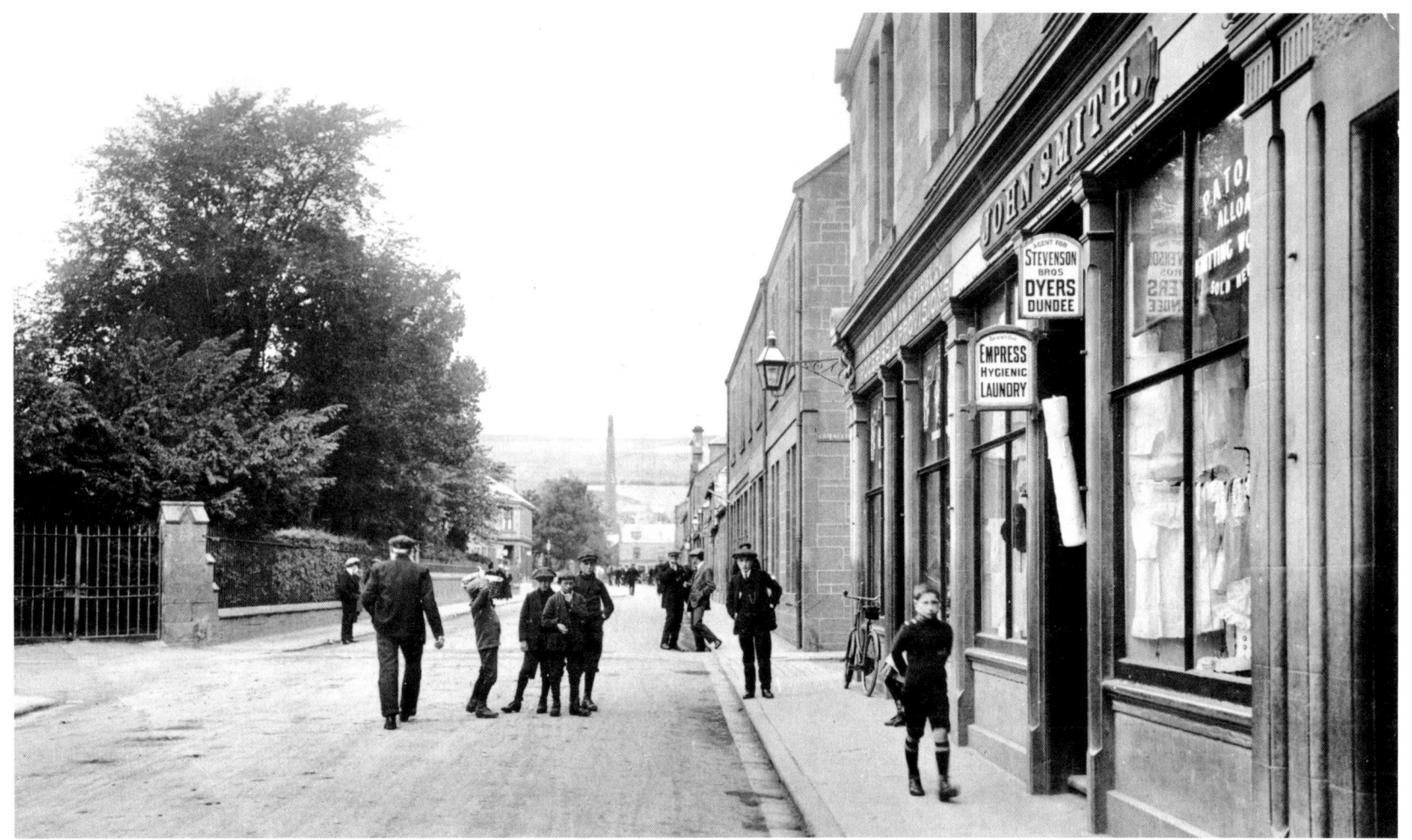

A little further south than the picture on the facing page, but still looking north, this view of Airlie Street shows it about 1914 at the intersection with Cairnleith Street on the right and St Ninian's Road on the left. Behind the trees on the left is St Ninian's Episcopal Church erected in 1856/57 to the designs of Edinburgh-based architect David Bryce. On the right are two prominent shops, Harry Dow's grocery and John Smith and Sons' drapery and outfitters. As is evident from the picture, Smith's also acted as laundry agents; customers would bring in their clothes, bedding and other items, it would be labelled and sometimes boxed, collected by vans, cleaned elsewhere at a large laundry facility and returned. A sign in Smith's window also indicates that customers could buy wool to knit their own garments.

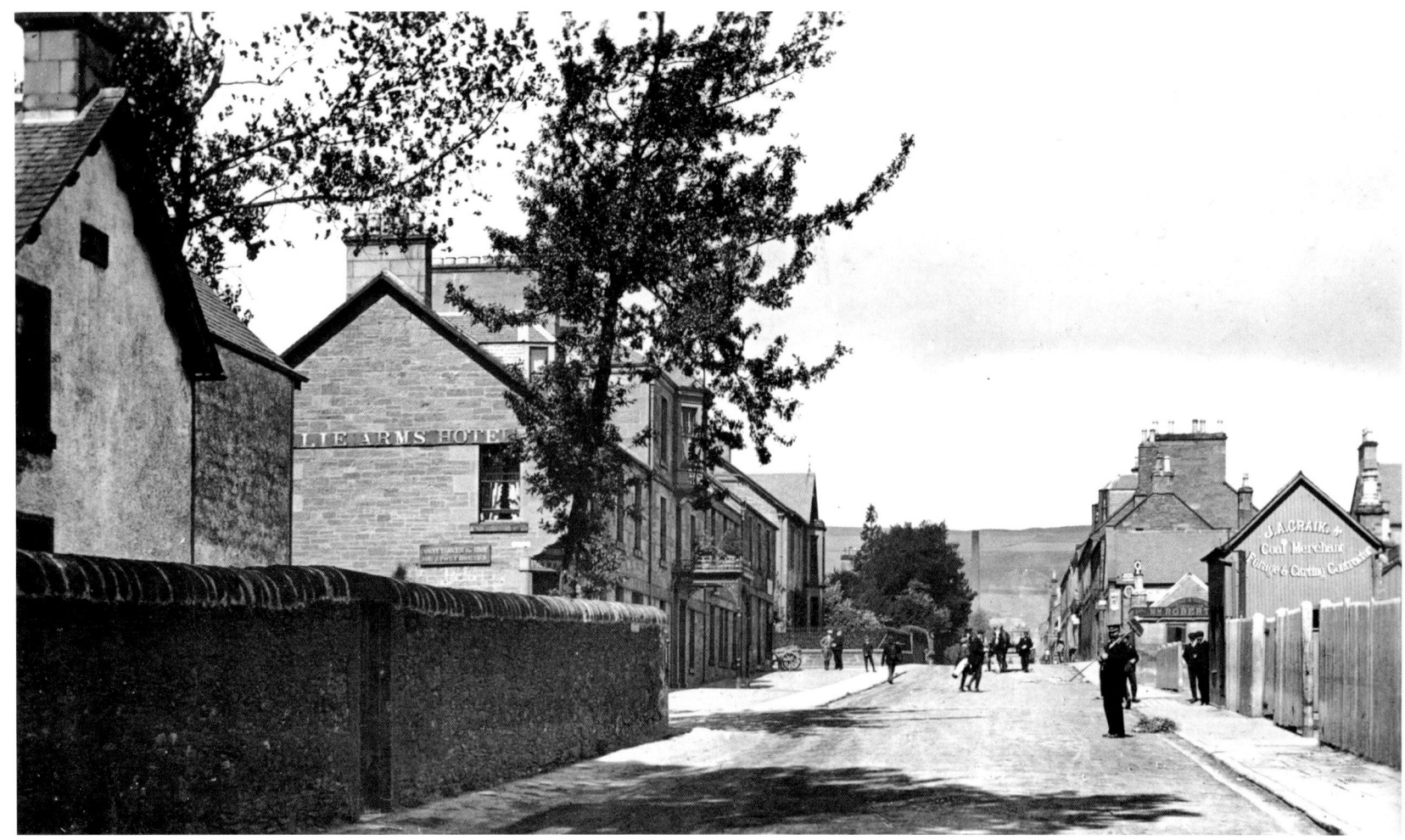

Half-hidden by the foreground wall and tree in this view is the Airlie Arms Hotel, which at the time the picture was taken around 1905, and for many years prior to that, was the premier hostelry for the area. It was well placed on Airlie Street, the main road into the town from the south with accommodation that was elegant and handsomely furnished, although in the days before en-suite facilities became the norm, bathrooms were separate. There was a billiard room and sporting guests could avail themselves of the excellent hunting, shooting and fishing on offer in the area. The hotel also had stables for residents' horses and kept post horses and carriages that people could hire for a tour of the country with drivers who were experienced, careful and familiar with all of the area's highways and byways.

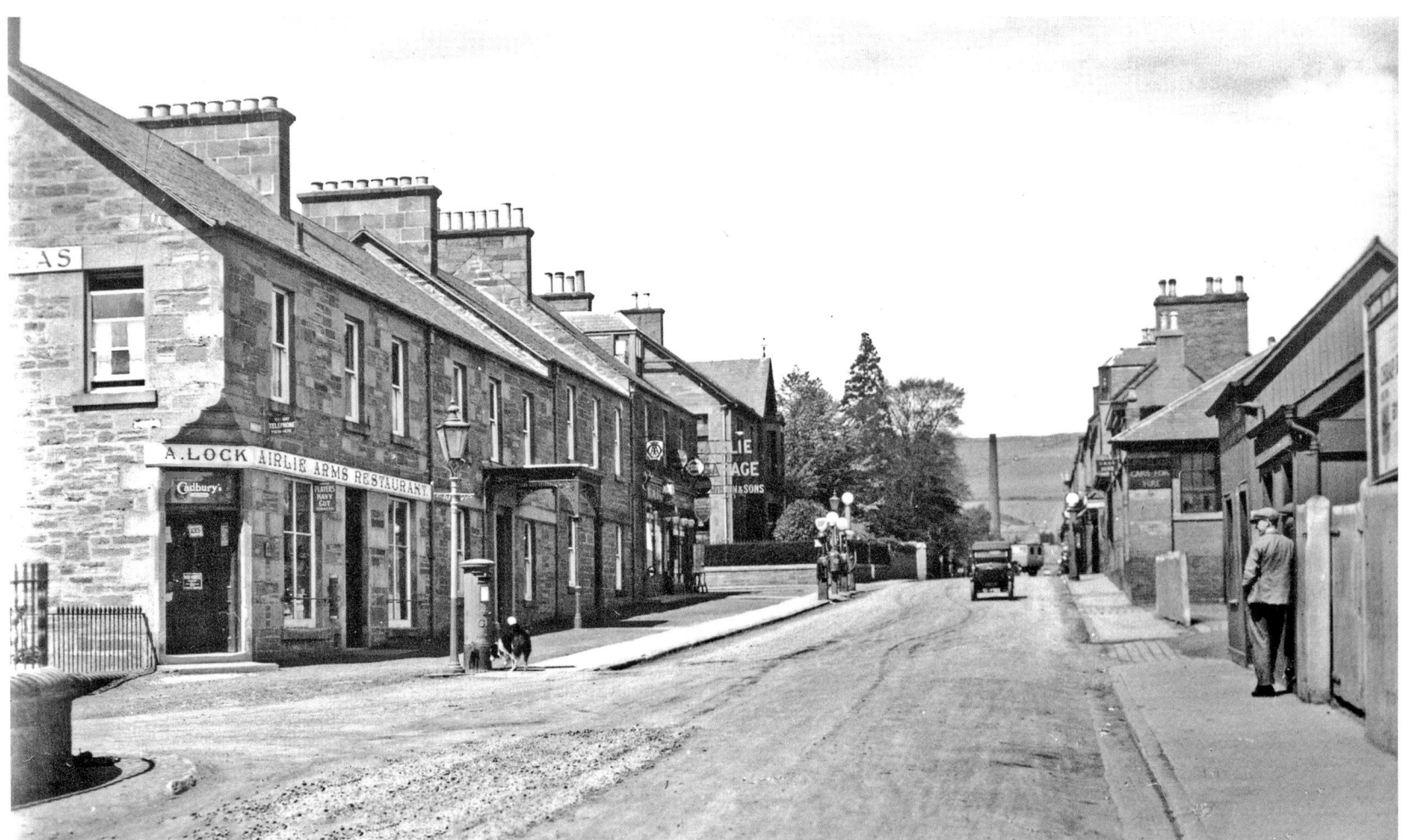

The Airlie Arms Hotel enjoyed one other advantage; just across the road was the railway station, which is also why a coal merchant's business can be seen opposite in the picture on the facing page. In this view, taken about twenty-five years later in 1930 and a little further north, the hotel sign has been replaced by one for the Airlie Arms Restaurant, perhaps a sign of changing times. One certain change is that horses, carriages and stables have been superseded by motor vehicles, with two garages, one owned by William McBain adjacent to the hotel building, faced by Alexander Edward's garage directly opposite on the east side of the street – petrol pumps can be seen in the middle distance on both sides of the street. William McBain resolved any problems when he bought out the competition.

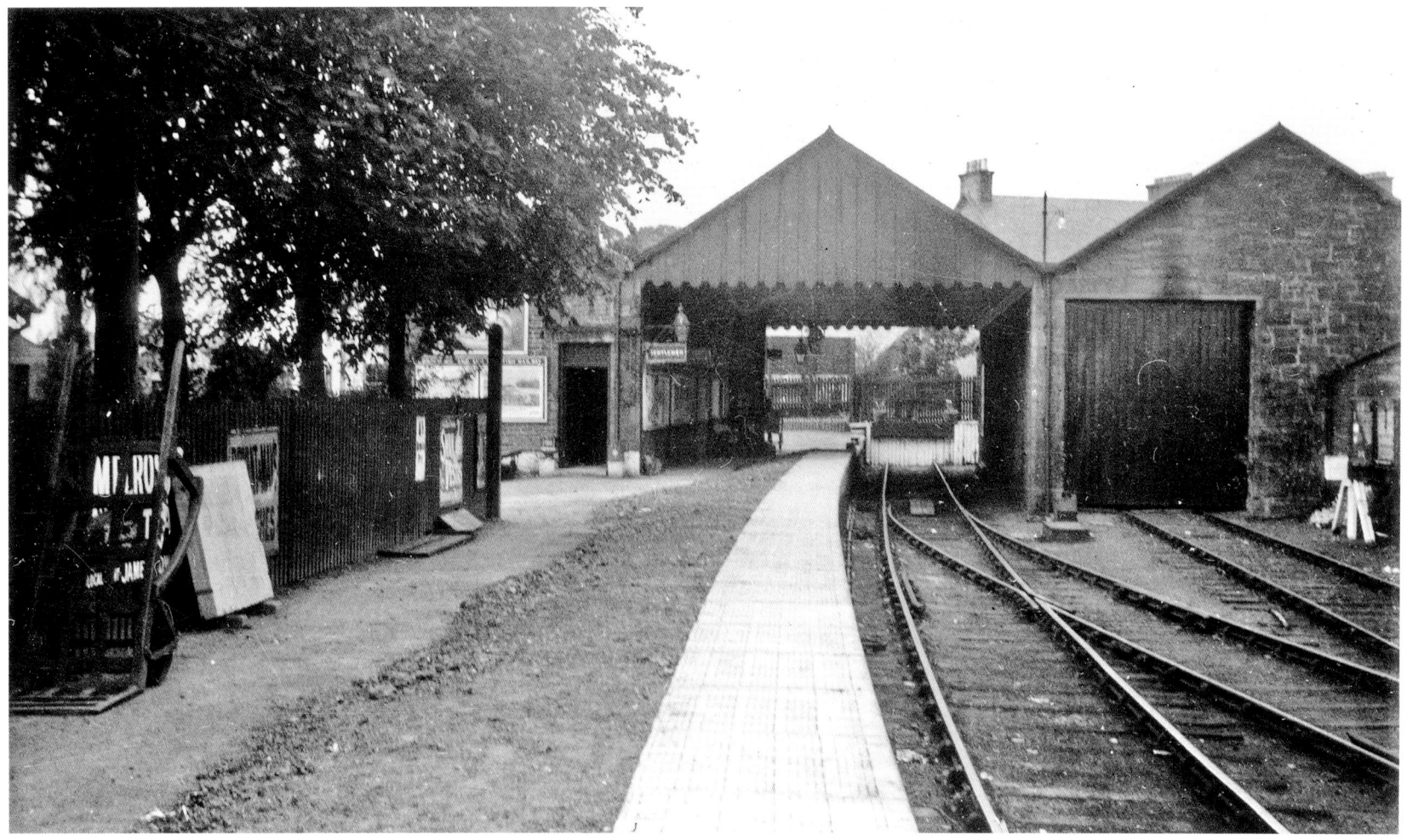

Alyth Station opened for passengers on 12th August 1861. The directors of the Alyth Railway Company, whose efforts culminated in the line been built, marked the occasion by travelling with their guests on a special train from Meigle, a journey that took about twenty minutes. The locomotive was decorated with evergreens and flowers, and flags waved from the carriage windows. A large crowd greeted the train on its arrival. After much cheering and waving, the directors, shareholders and friends then went to the industrial school for refreshments and congratulatory speech making. Expectations were high that with the town now served by a railway the people of Dundee would flock to see the dramatic Highland scenery, the beautiful Loch of Lintrathen and spectacular Reekie Linn waterfall. Alyth had become a tourist destination.

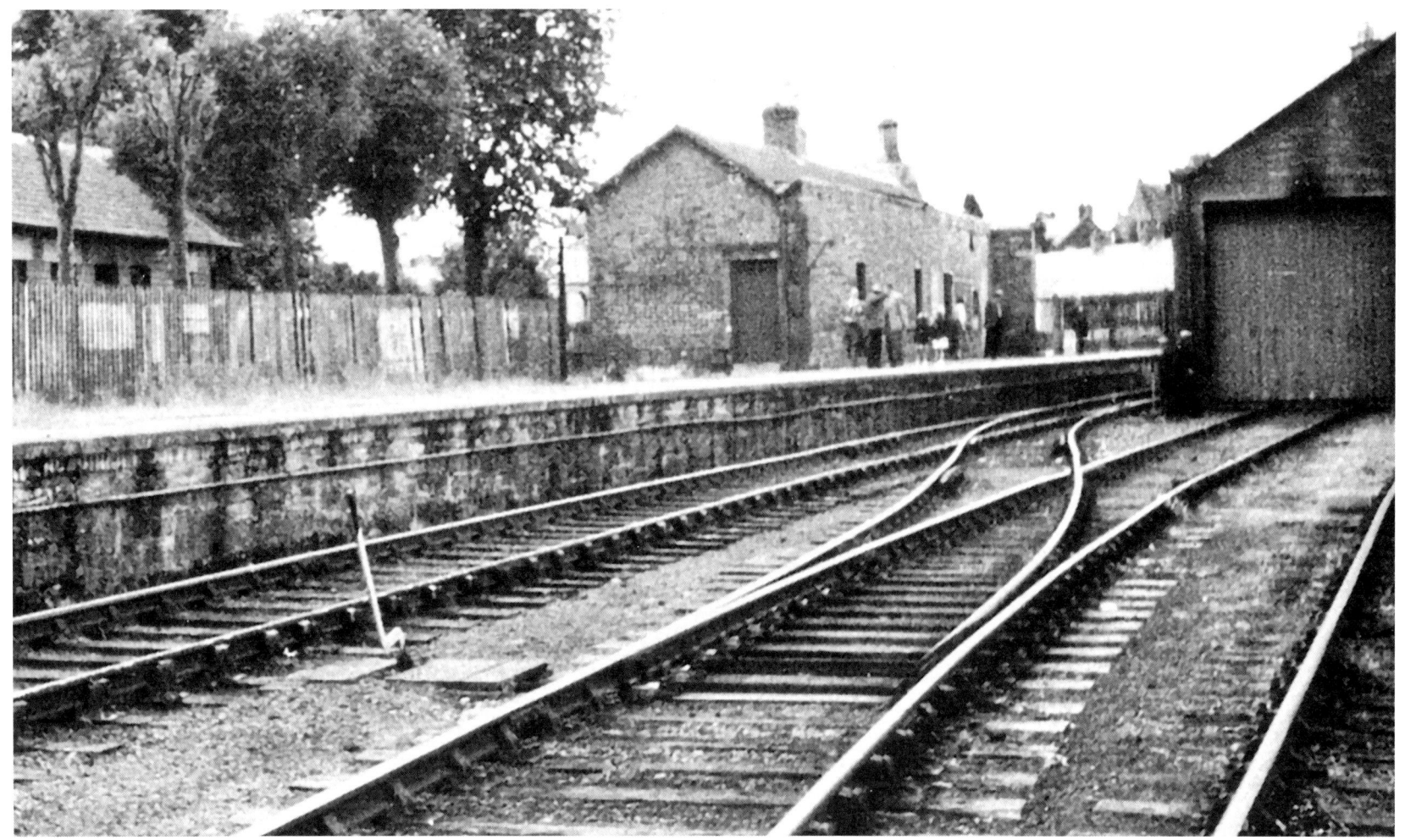

Carrying goods was always the main revenue earner for railways and for a while before the arrival of the first passenger train, goods trains had been making the run to Alyth. Bolstering the local textile mills, delivering coal, moving agricultural produce and carrying livestock to and from market were the principal reasons for building the railway, but passenger services had value too. The station was a single platform terminus with a roof spanning the end of the line between the station building and goods shed as seen in the picture on the facing page. It had been removed before the cessation of passenger services on 2nd July 1951 and is clearly missing from this picture taken during a visit by railway enthusiasts who arrived by special train in 1960, which they could do because the line remained open for goods traffic until 1st March 1965.

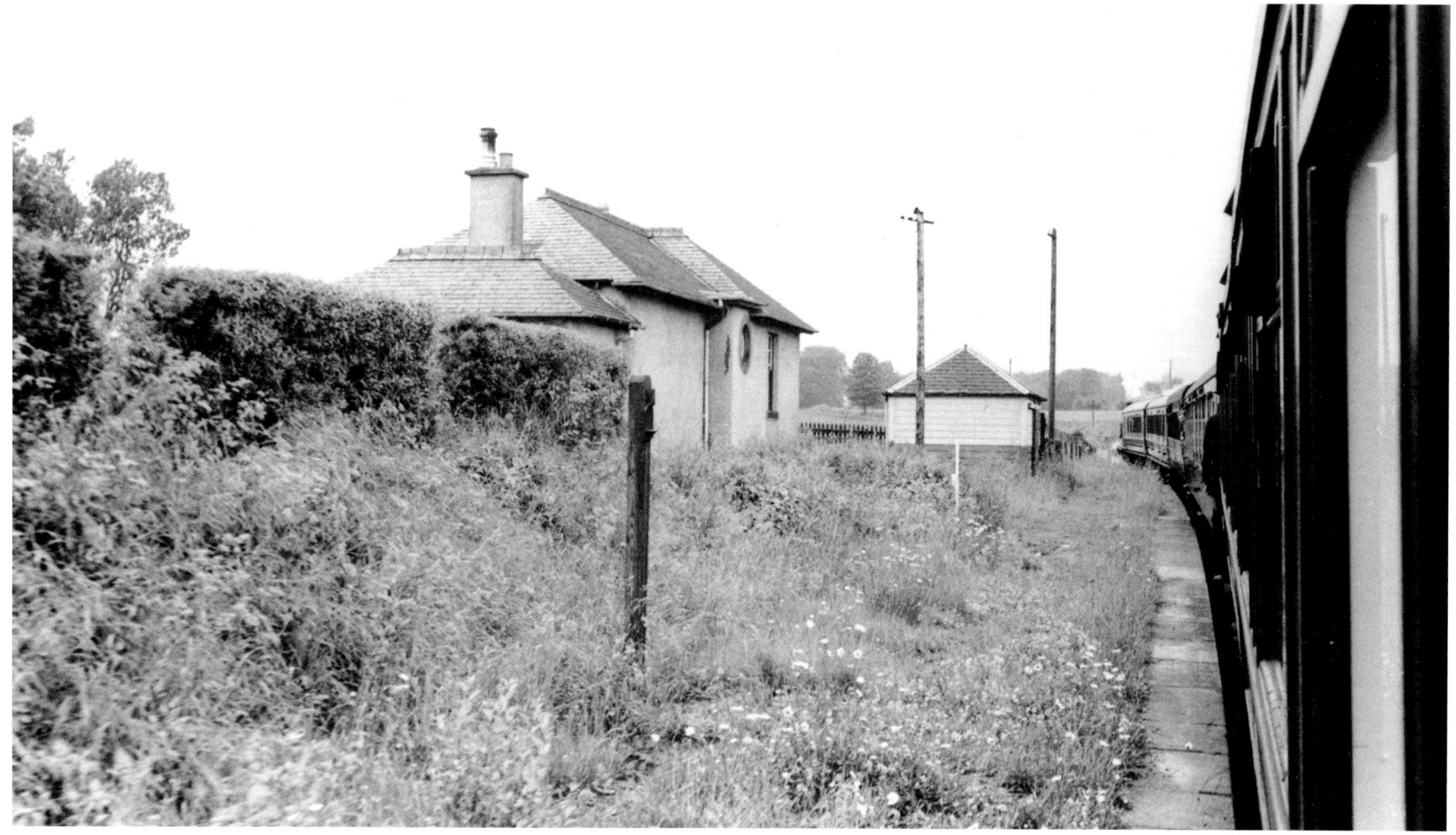

The line from Meigle was not much more than four miles long, but the engineers had to bridge the Dean Water and River Isla at Cardean close to the site of a Roman camp, and dig a long cutting through hard rock at Jordanstone where an intermediate station was sited. It is looking a little forlorn in this picture taken from the enthusiasts' train in 1960. At the time the line opened in the 1860s the country was caught up in a fever of big railway companies absorbing smaller ones. One of the main players, the Glasgow-based Caledonian Railway, took over all the lines in and around Strathmore including the Alyth branch. At some point that company's deputy chairman acquired Cardean as his country estate and when the 'Caley' built a crack main-line express locomotive in 1906, they called it *Cardean*, so a name from beside the little Alyth railway could be seen speeding between Glasgow and Carlisle, and beyond!

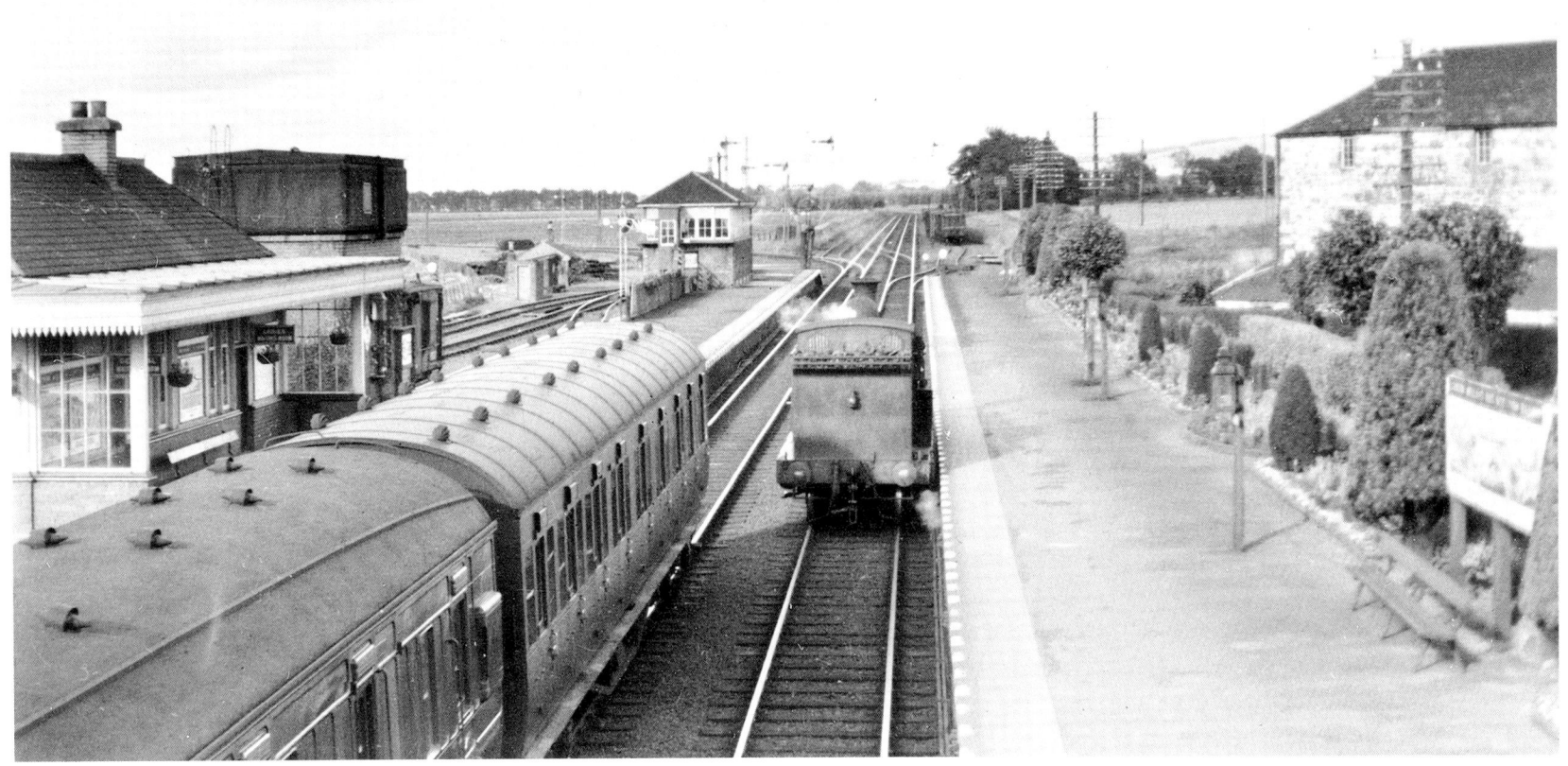

Railway development throughout the country was piecemeal. The main Strathmore Railway from Perth to Forfar was opened in 1848 by the Scottish Midland Junction Railway. With the Arbroath and Forfar Railway and the Aberdeen Railway, which opened in 1854, they formed a route between Perth and Aberdeen. Two years later the three companies amalgamated as the Scottish North Eastern Railway which lasted until 1866 when it was absorbed into the Caledonian Railway. A feature of the line through Strathmore was the number of branch railways, including that to Alyth, linking it to places on either side. Railway practice usually meant that the junction of these lines was named after the destination of the branch, so Alyth Junction Station was actually about five miles south of the town. It is seen here in 1950 looking east with the line to and from Alyth heading off to the left, just beyond the signal box. Meigle was the first station about a mile to the north of the junction and to the south another branch was formed where it met the remarkable pioneering Dundee to Newtyle Railway, which opened in 1831 and was re-engineered in the 1860s adding complexity to the junction.

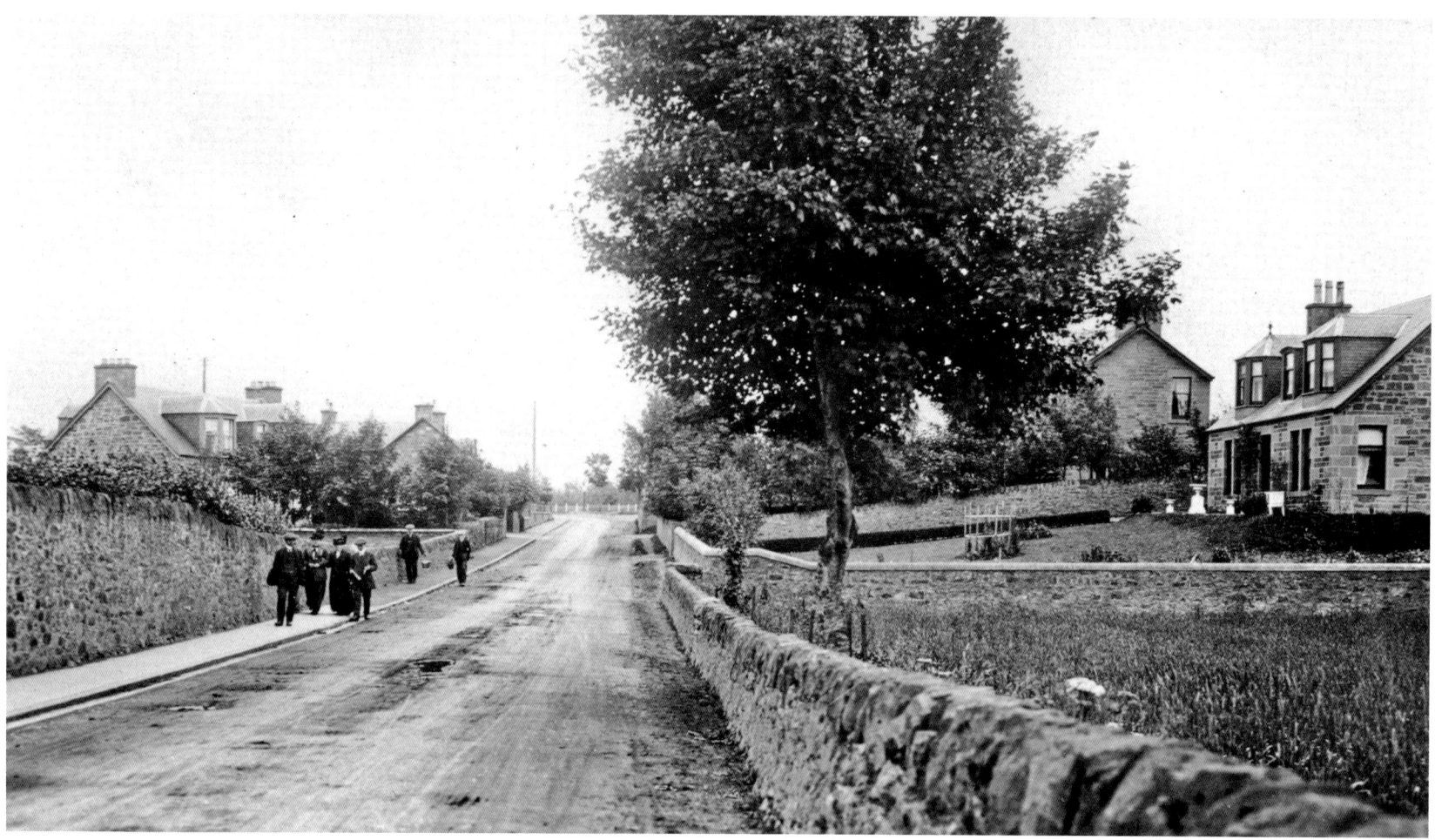

The railway station was situated at the southern edge of the town, so almost inevitably the town shifted southwards with housing developments along South Airlie Street as shown in this picture from about 1914. Business and commerce also developed with the Meigle and Alyth Auction Mart Company setting up their premises at the road end and erecting animal pens on the Market Muir. Livestock sales were held at set dates in the year and sales of agricultural produce took place at other times. When a farm or associated business hit hard times, the auctioneers could be called on to conduct a displenishing sale of their animals, poultry, crops, machinery and other moveable assets. The mart was also used for non-agricultural purposes as in 1916 when a free gift sale of donated items raised funds to help the British Red Cross Society in their work during a war that was to have a more permanent reminder on the Market Muir.

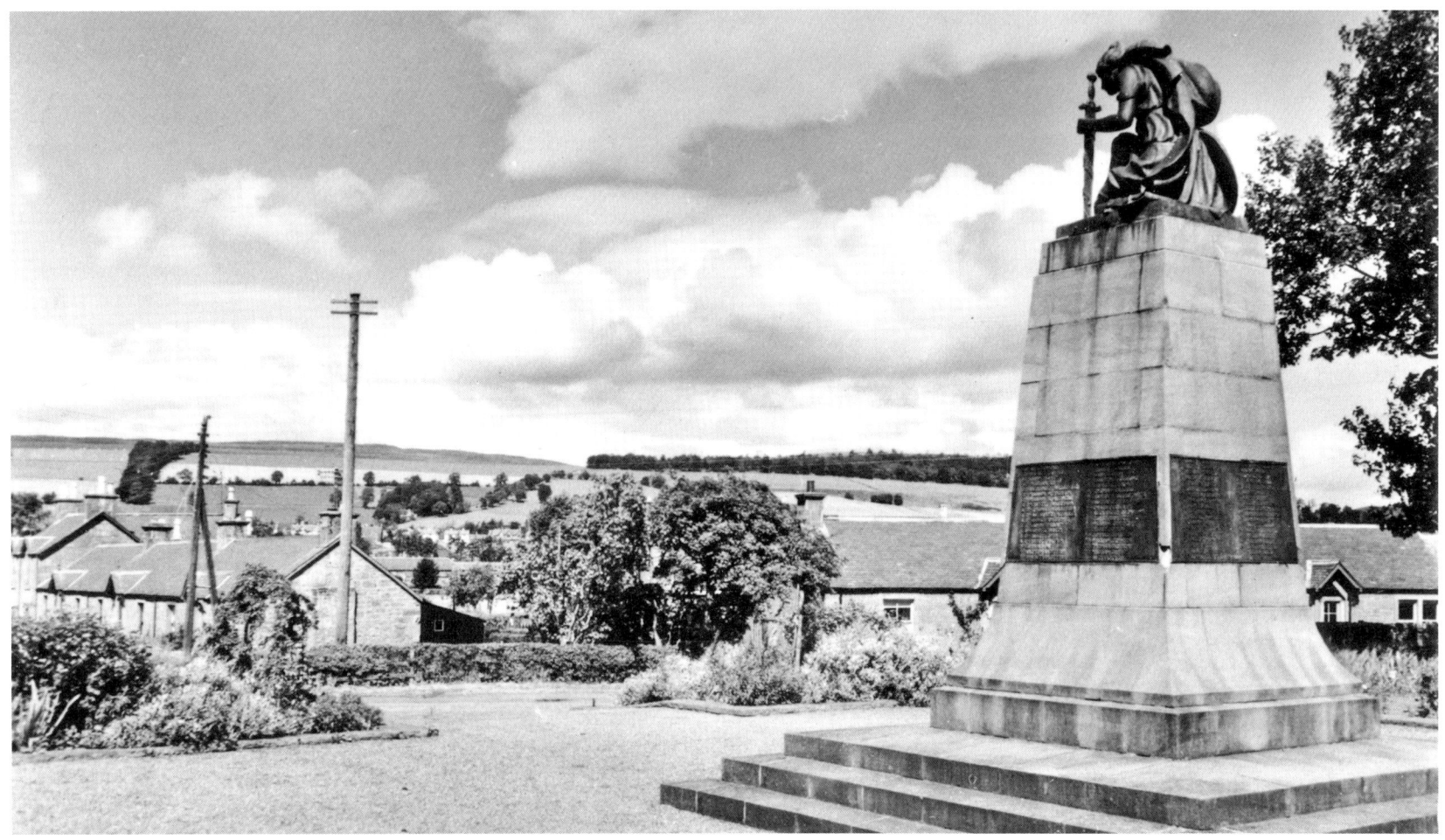

In July 1922, 21 years after the memorial to the South African War had been erected, a procession formed up in Market Square to walk to the Market Muir. There, a winged victory statue mounted on a pedestal of Camperdown stone had been erected as a memorial to the men of the district who had lost their lives in the First World War. About 1,000 people, including members of public bodies, schoolchildren, Girl Guides, Scouts, Cubs, boys of the Boys' Brigade, the Alyth Silver Band, former servicemen and the public took part. At the memorial, two local former soldiers in Black Watch uniform mounted a guard of honour. The Provost introduced the 10th Earl of Airlie who, after paying tribute to the fallen, unveiled the statue. Pipe Major Lamond of Newtyle played the *Flowers o' the Forest*, buglers sounded the *Last Post* and *Reveille* and members of the various groups and public laid wreaths in a solemn ceremony curtailed, but perhaps made more poignant, by rain.

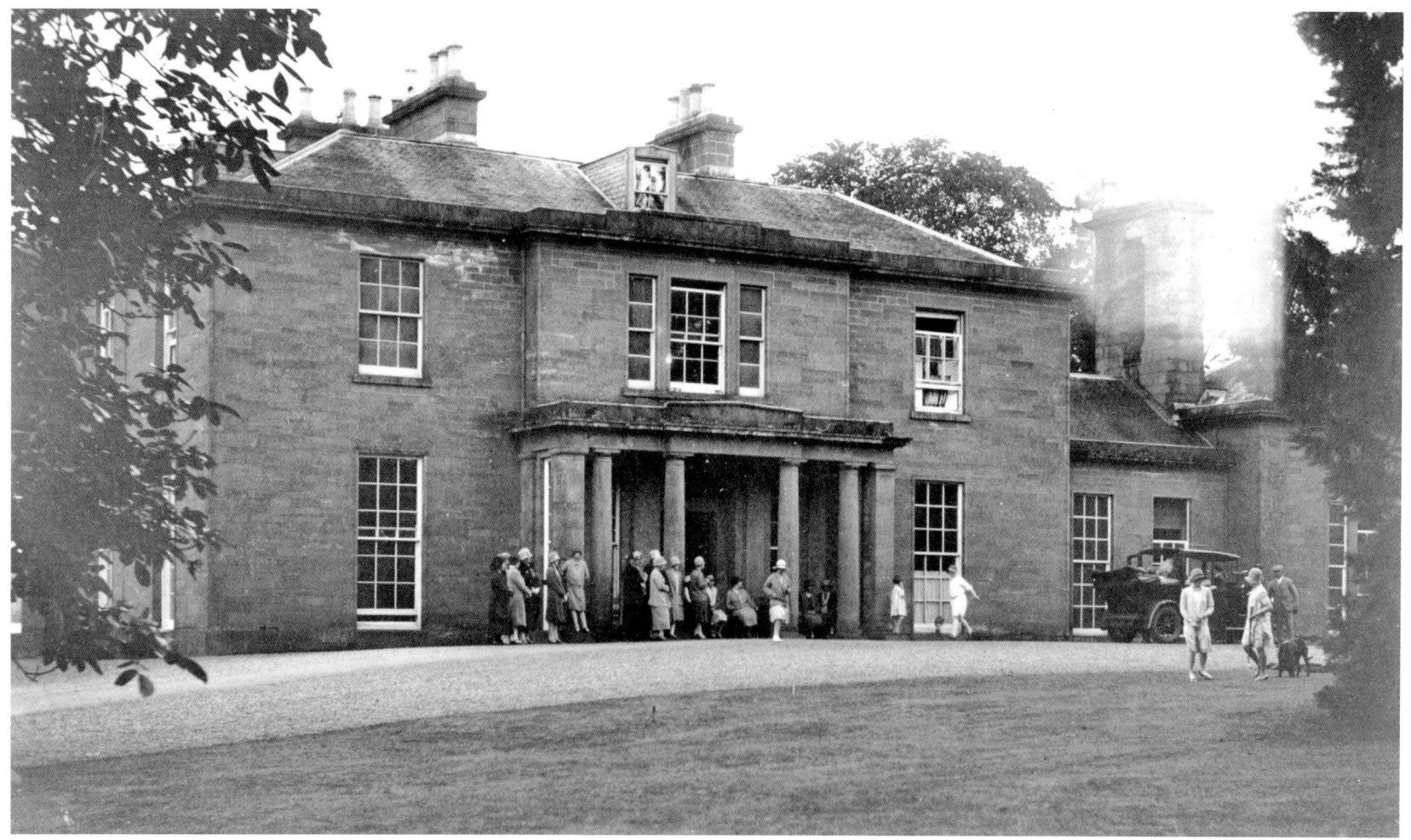

The First World War memorial on Market Muir was augmented some years later with another to commemorate the Second World War, a conflict that took on a different aspect for the local area when a prisoner of war camp was set up at Balhary. Identified as Camp No.63, it housed mainly Italian men who worked on local farms. The camp was a short distance from Balhary House, a neat Georgian mansion situated about a mile south of the Market Muir. It was built in 1817/1821 to the designs of architect and surveyor John Carver for lawyer John Smyth whose descendant, Mr A. G. Kinloch-Smyth, along with the Earl of Airlie gifted the Den of Alyth to the town. The hats and clothes of the women gathering outside suggest that this photo of the house dates from about 1930.

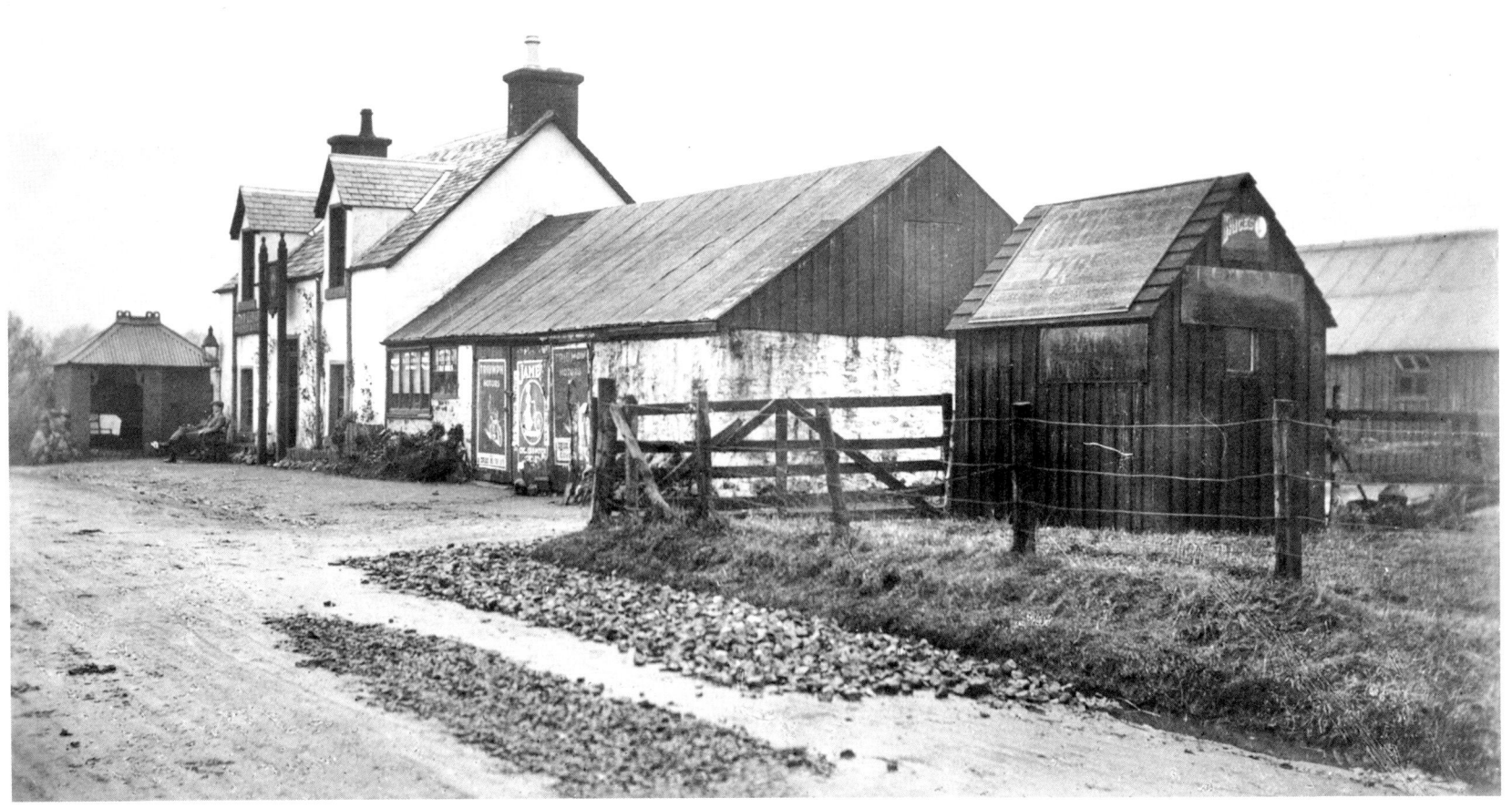

A demure social gathering, like that on the facing page, was unlikely to be hosted at the building featured in this undated picture. Known as 'The Blackbird' and set beside the Blairgowrie Road a short distance to the west of Market Muir, it has been a roadside inn for a long time. In 1882 the outbuildings caught fire, killing a milk cow and pigs, which suggests that the inn may at that time have served produce from its own animals and adjacent fields. That incident predated this picture, which shows the house and outbuildings looking decidedly rural. Since then the Blackbird Inn has been significantly expanded as a pub, restaurant and meeting place. The road has been much improved from the ill-made muddy track that appears here, the trees have grown a bit and a caravan park was opened alongside. The inn sits on the edge of the little planned village of New Alyth, which was set out on a grid pattern in 1833.

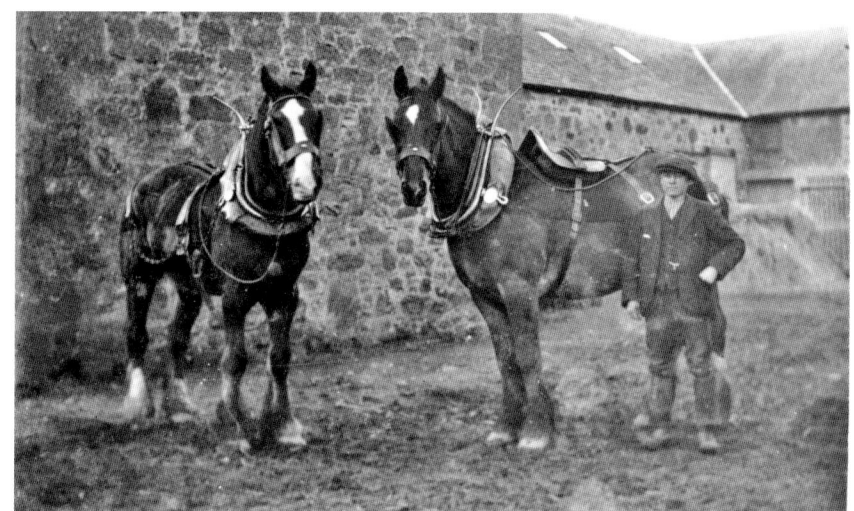
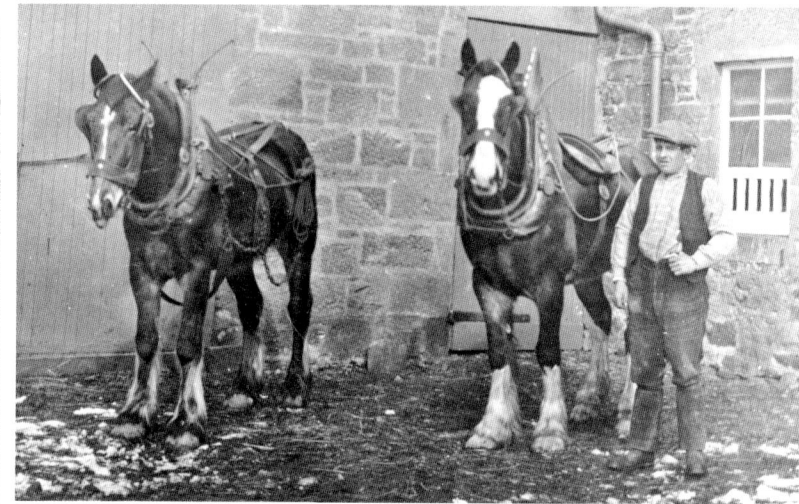
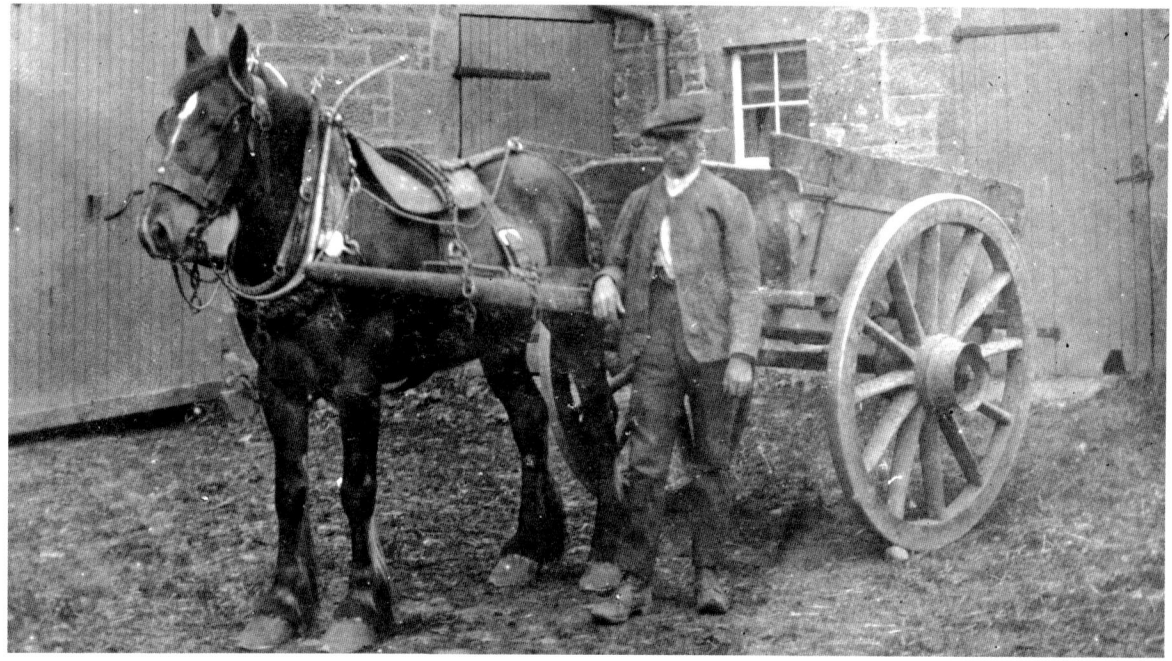

The magnificent horses, shown on these pages with their handlers, once typified farming life in the area. On this page the top left picture shows Alex Penman at Aberbothrie in 1922. The pictures on the right were taken at Burnside Farm in 1921 and show Alistair Ritchie with a working pair (*upper*) and Dan McLean with horse and cart (*lower*). On the facing page Alex Grant is ploughing at Bankhead in 1918. Majestic heavy horses like these always evoke a special image of the countryside, although these photos also show the reality of hard work and a tough life far removed from the romantic idyll often associated with such creatures. These were working horses, but such animals could on occasions be given a full wash and brush-up, fitted with polished harness and presented at the Stormont and Strathmore Agricultural Show or the later Alyth Horse Show.

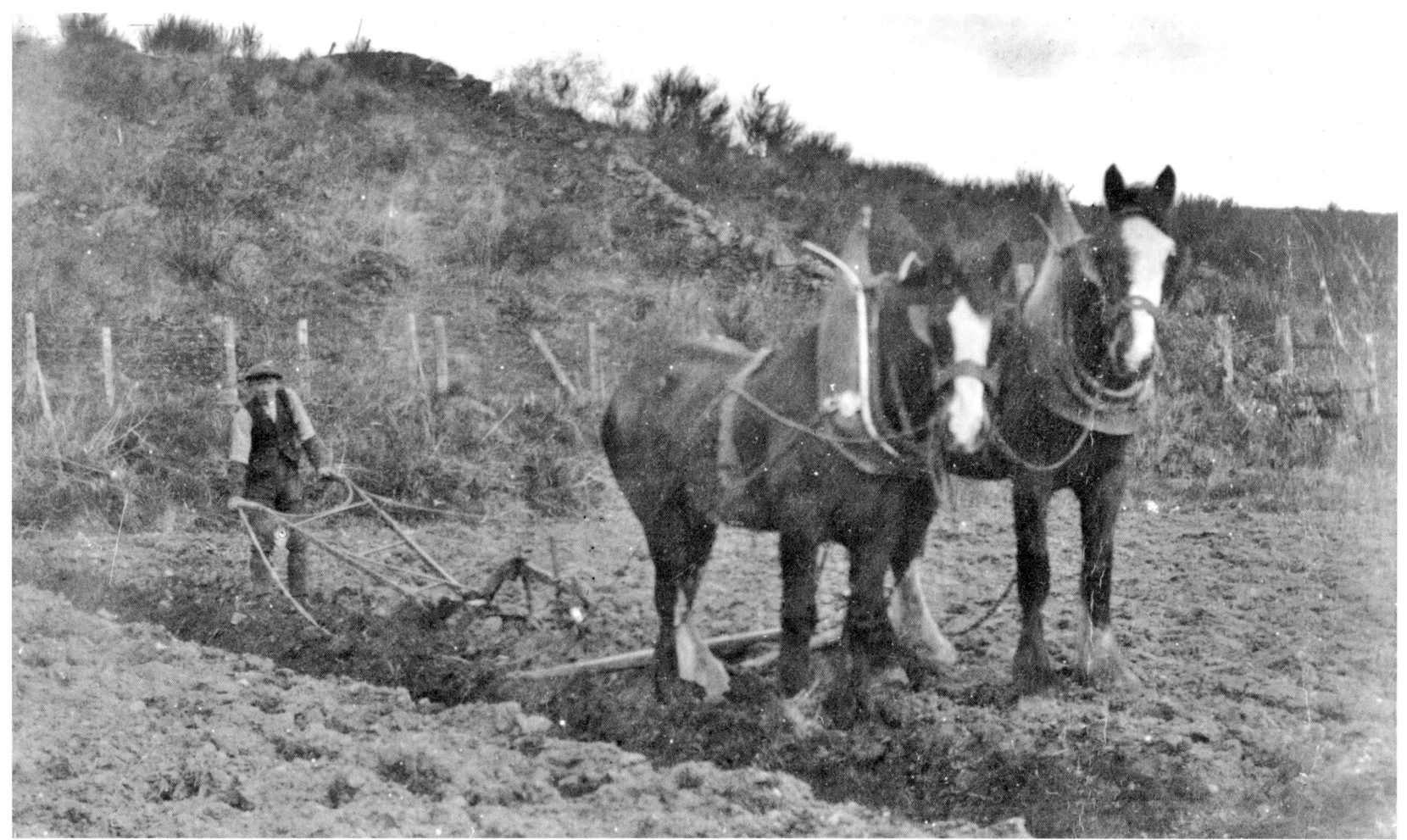

The Alyth Horse Show was held for many years at the Diamond Jubilee Park, a splendid recreational facility gifted to the town by the Earl of Airlie and opened in October 1898. A parade made up of floats and bands formed up at the Market Muir and processed to the new park where speeches were given and tributes made to 'The Bonnie Hoose o' Airlie'. The annual show was a big occasion for the town and it wasn't restricted to equine exhibits as there were other activities like sheep shearing, and races on foot or bicycle. Prizes were awarded for horses and harness, but also for produce and smaller creatures like rabbits, dogs or poultry. A particularly big show was held in 1951, the Festival of Britain year, but only a couple of years later a tractor stole the show as young farmers queued up to pay a shilling to test their skills at driving a tractor and trailer: change was coming to the farming world!

The countryside around Alyth was full of contrasts, because set amongst the working farms were a number of grand mansions and estates, complete with imposing gates, driveways and lodges. One such, lying to the west of Alyth close to Burnside and Aberbothrie farms, was Greymount House. It was a mansion of three public rooms, six bedrooms, usual offices, greenhouse, garage, orchard garden and grounds, 51 acres of farmland and a lodge of three rooms.

On Alyth's east side, Balloch House was a close neighbour of Bankhead Farm. Like Loyal House and Alyth Town Hall, it was designed by architect Andrew Heiton and built in 1877 consisting of four reception rooms, five bedrooms, offices, servant's quarters, garage, greenhouse and well laid out garden grounds.

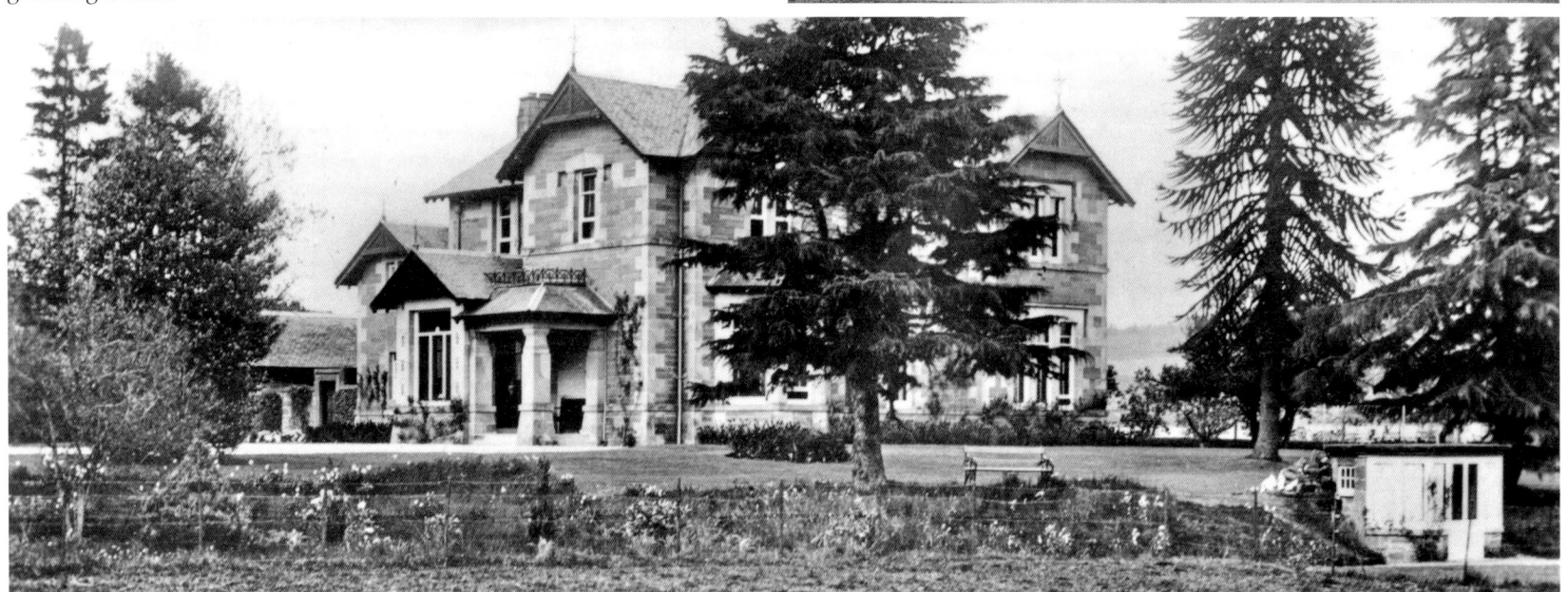

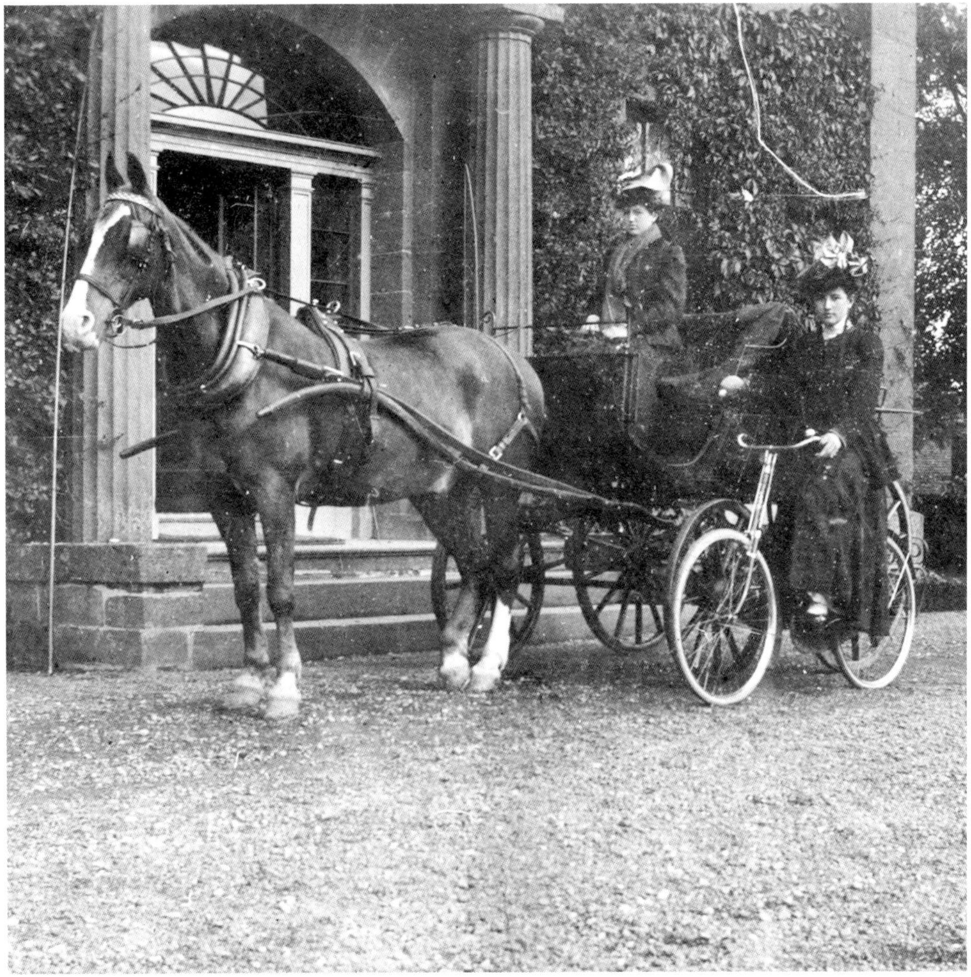

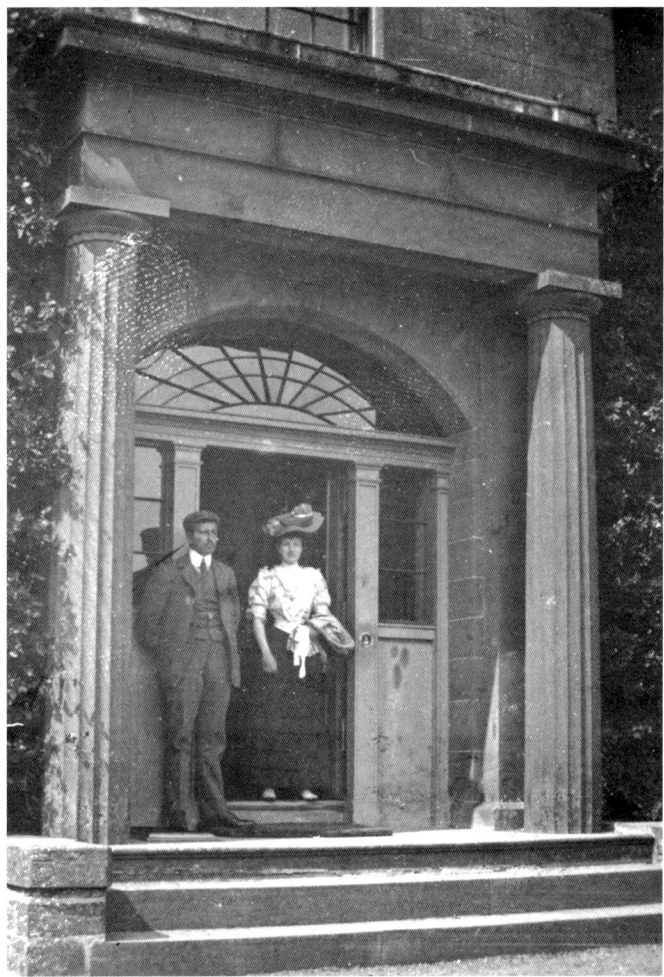

A couple of miles south of Alyth is Bardmony House, another of the area's country mansions, but one that incorporated an earlier structure from the fourteenth or fifteenth century, so the site has a history of occupancy. The house is seen here in 1906 with the occupants or visitors posing with transport options outside the front door. The Greek Doric columns flanking the portico with its elegant Georgian fanlight are part of the building as remodelled in 1830 when it contained a drawing room, study, dining room, five bedrooms, ancillary rooms, the usual offices, kitchen, cellar and attic. There were outbuildings with stables and other functions, lawns, a walled garden and wooded policies, everything the small country estate would want, although a west wing was added in 1991.

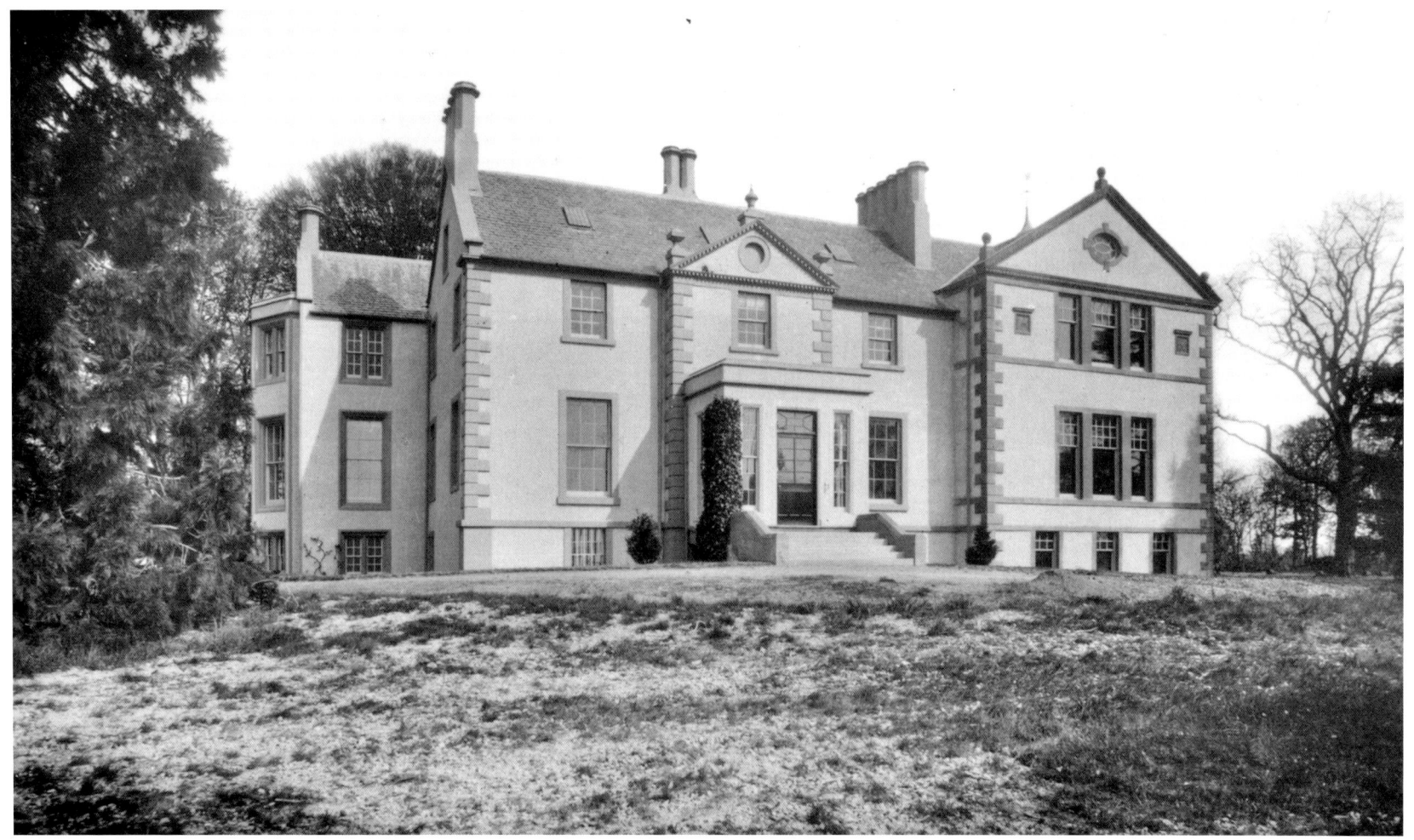

The first part of Jordanstone House, to the south east of Alyth, was built in the late eighteenth century. It was a small house with a projecting central section topped by classical pediment. It was extended in 1890 when the wing on the right of the picture was added to the original. When a matching wing was built on the left in 1929, the structure regained its symmetry. The Jordanstone name has become widely familiar because of James Duncan, who made a fortune from trading and, when he died in 1909, left a bequest of £60,000 to establish a school of industrial art in Dundee, unusually also stipulating that women should be educated at the institution. After resolving legal matters, the Duncan of Jordanstone College of Art was opened in the 1930s and has become one of the country's foremost art and design schools and part of the University of Dundee.

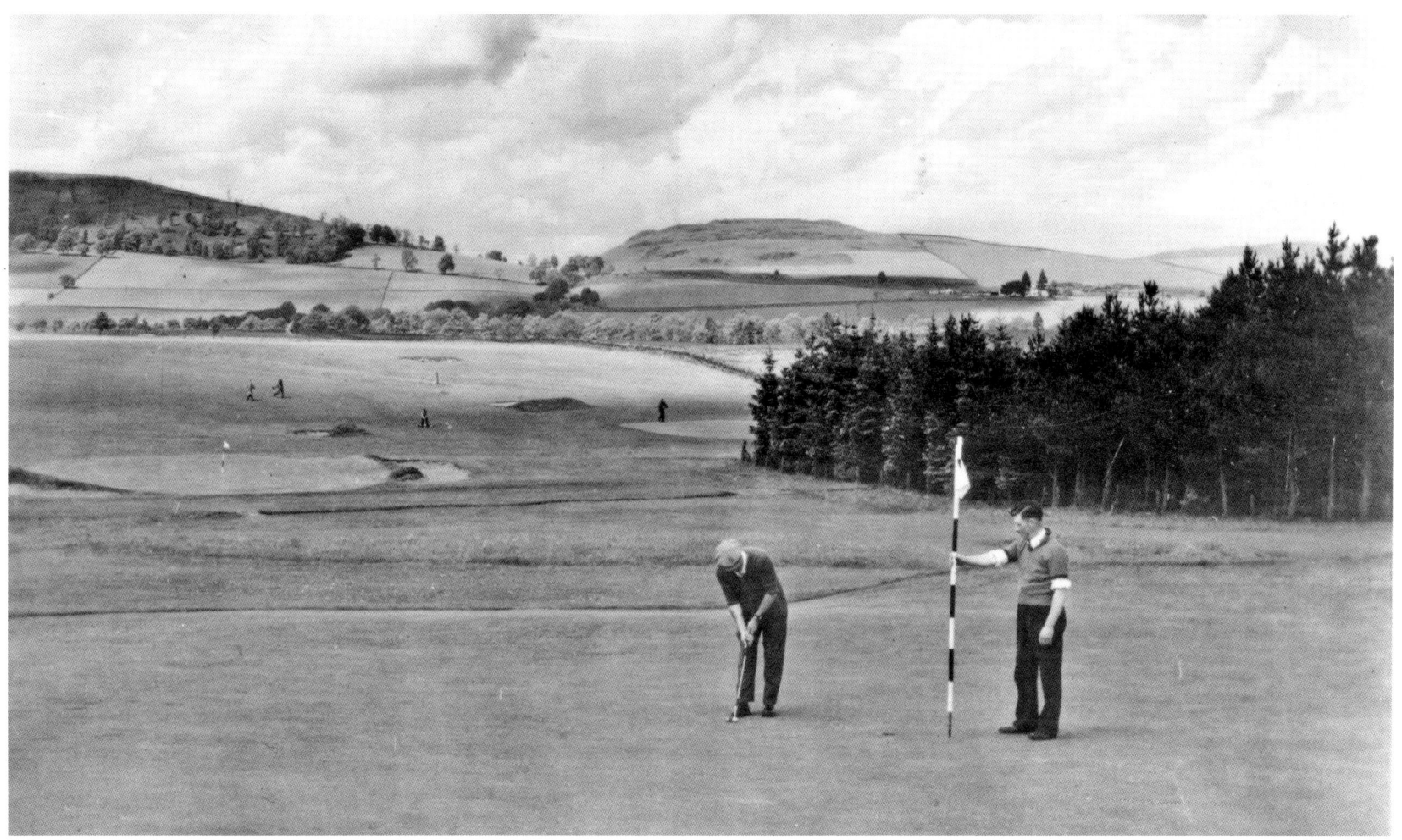

Situated to the east of the town at Pitcrocknie, Alyth Golf Club was formed in 1894 with a nine hole course laid out by old Tom Morris, the great course designer from St Andrews in Fife. It was expanded to eighteen holes in the 1930s by that other master of course design from Fife, James Braid of Elie. Playing to over 6,000 yards and the opposite of a flat-track links, where distance is paramount, a more accurate game was needed to meet the challenge of the hilly course. Laid out on moorland turf that made for excellent fairways, the course is blessed with other natural delights including a wide variety of trees, heather and glorious scenery, although being distracted by views or lulled by the peaceful surroundings might not be ideal for a golfer trying to improve their handicap.

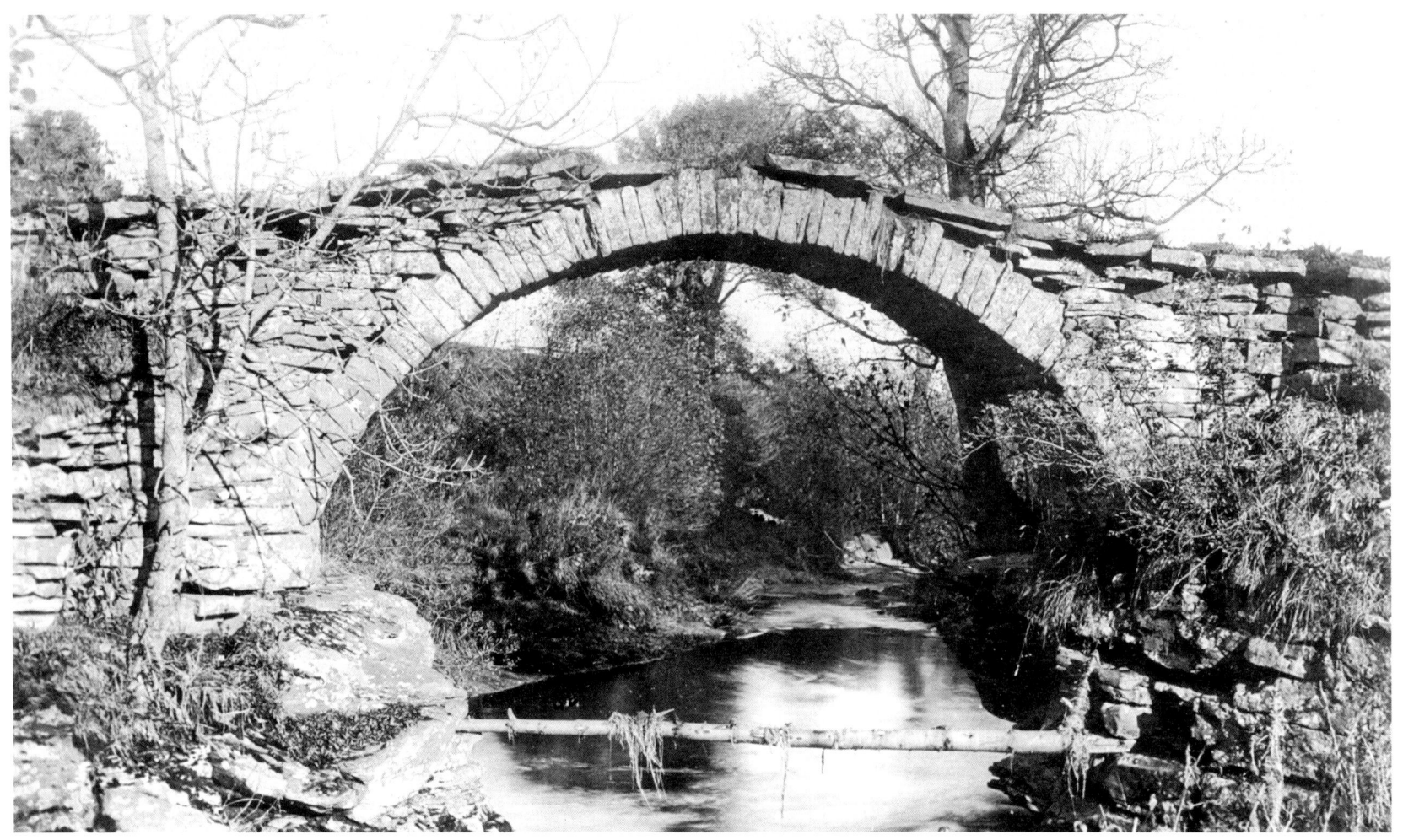

As the Alyth Burn flows east, it is spanned by the Bridge of Ruim, sometimes referred to as the Brig o' Rome, a usage that makes it sound older than its early eighteenth century date. A relic of the days when the only way to get goods around the country was by packhorse, it had a very narrow deck and no parapets. Before the Alyth Burn flows into the River Isla its name changes to the River, or Burn, of Quiech and at the confluence, on a steep bank above the Isla, are the ruins of Inverquiech Castle. An ancient fortress possibly dating from the late twelfth century, it was there in 1296 when King Edward I stayed for a night, while burnishing his reputation as the 'Hammer of the Scots'. Later, the castle was deliberately destroyed and then rebuilt before falling into ruin and providing local people with a handy source of building stone.